D1211389

COME SHARE
THE
BEING

COME SHARE
THE
BEING

" You may come to share in the very being of God "

Bob Benson

**impact
books**

Library of Congress Catalog Card Number: 74-83412
ISBN 0-914850-94-6

FIRST EDITION

ACKNOWLEDGEMENTS

Dow Jones-Irwin, Inc., Homewood, Illinois for **Struggle For Identity** by Roger D'Aprix. Copyright © 1972 by Dow Jones-Irwin, Inc. Used by permission.

E. P. Dutton & Co., Inc., New York, for **The World of Pooh** by A. A. Milne. Copyright © 1957 by E. P. Dutton & Co., Inc. Used by permission.

Harper and Row Publishers, New York, for "Dudley Pippin and The Principal" from **Dudley Pippin** by Phil Reasoner. Copyright © 1965 by Phil Reasoner. Used by permission of the publisher.

Harper and Row Publishers, New York, for **The Art of Loving** by Erich Fromm. Copyright © 1956 by Erich Fromm. Used by permission of the publisher.

Harper and Row Publishers, New York, for **The Knowledge of The Holy** by A. W. Tozer. Copyright © 1961 by A. W. Tozer. Used by permission of the publisher.

Harper and Row Publishers, New York, for **We The Lonely People** by Ralph Keyes. Copyright © 1973 by Ralph Keyes. Used by permission of the publisher.

Impact Books, Nashville, Tennessee, for **I'm Out To Change My World** by Ann Kiemel. Copyright © 1974 by Impact Books.

Impact Books, Nashville, Tennessee, for **We Really Do Need Each Other** by Reuben Welch. Copyright © 1973 by Impact Books.

Me-Books Publishing Company, N. Hollywood, California, for **My Friendly Giraffe,** a Me-Book publication. Copyright © 1972 by Me-Books, A division of Dart Direct Merchandising Corporation. Used by permission.

The **New English Bible** for passages from "II Peter" and the "Gospel Of John". Copyright © The Delegates of the Oxford University Press and Syndics of the Cambridge University Press 1961, 1970. Used by permission.

Open Court Publishing Company, LaSalle, Illinois, for **Meetings** by Martin Buber. Copyright © 1973 by Library of Living Philosophers. Used by permission of the publishers.

Fleming H. Revell Company, Old Tappan, New Jersey, for **Love Is Something You Do** by Frederick B. Speakman. Copyright © 1959 by Fleming H. Revell. Used by permission.

dedicated to my family—
where learning to do is easy—
you get drowned out or
left behind if you don't
and where learning to be is important-
to find that which is really you
and which is yours to share.

Contents

CHAPTER I

CHAPTER I

I Believe

I've lain in the grass on a soft spring morning
with life chirping and buzzing about me
      and these were the things
          I said to the buttercups and crocuses
             and sang to the robins.
I've walked into a dimly-lit room at night
illuminated only by the rays of a Donald Duck night light
      and these were the things
          I whispered over the sleeping forms
          of my little boys.
I was out to the edge for a moment once—
out where they say you have something
we don't have a cure for
          and faced with separation from loved ones,
             with uncompleted tasks and unfulfilled dreams
      these were the things that brought me
      warm hope and comfort.
These are the things I believe about God.

I'm more than just toenails and whiskers and elbows
      and a social security number

way down deep inside these things pull me together
and make me a "me."
I am the measure of the truth I have adopted
and I have believed these things
until there is no distance between me and them.
One by one, I have stripped away doubts
and questions
until I have possessed these truths
and they have possessed me.

And if you could put your ear
up tight against my heart
when trials and darkness have stilled me to a whisp
or if you were there when joy burst forth
in such loud song that you had to back away—
These are the things you would he
from my voice and
from my very being.
These are the things that are really me
they are the things I believe
about God.

CHAPTER II

CHAPTER II

"God Is A Bummer"

She looked at me across the table and casually but honestly and firmly said, "God is a bummer." And if the story she told me was fair and true and an honest appraisal of her life so far she may have even had some right to think it or feel it. Except that it is very important what we think about God.

A. W. Tozer, the great Christian believer and preacher, said in his book, *The Knowledge of The Holy,* "What comes into our minds when we think about God is the most important thing about us...and the most portentous fact about any man is not what he at a given time may say or do, but what he in his deep heart conceives God to be like." And he goes on to say, "That our idea of God correspond as nearly as possible to the true being of God is of immense importance to us."

During an illness some months ago I was listening to a new album by a group called "The Truth." And on that album there was a musical setting of my creed:

> *"God is so good*
> *God is so good*
> *God is so good*
> *He's so good to me."*

And when I am lonely or discouraged or blue or perplexed or bewildered or bursting with joy — I don't recite the Nicene Creed or the Athanasian Creed or the Apostle's Creed or even the first fourteen pages of the church manual. I believe all that stuff, but mostly I sing

**"God is so good,
He's so good to me."**

I believe that He is so good that He doesn't even care if someone in all honesty or candor questions His integrity or even accuses Him of being "a bummer" —

He is so good.

In the last few months in our College Sunday School class we have been studying a passage, or mostly a phrase from II Peter. In the New English Bible it is translated like this:

*And through these promises,
great beyond all price…
— you may come to share
in the very being of God.*

And together we have been trying to define "the very being of God." In the King James' it speaks of being made "partakers of the nature of God." But somehow it seems stronger to think of what we might be

if we *"shared in the very being of God."*

Sometimes the thought that we are made in the image of God comes to us. But mostly when we think of images we think of look-alikes. I went to see an old man the other day who had known me since I was born. He had cut my hair in his basement when I ran around with his son. I think he is in his eighties and he can hardly see. In fact, he couldn't even see the chair and we had to aim him to get him in it. And he said to me, "Bob, you look more like your dad everyday." Well, everybody knows I have always been better looking than my dad, he just had his images mixed up.

It's funny, when our first son, Bob, Jr., was born, we thought, at the time, that he was the most beautiful baby that had ever been born…just outstanding. But by the time he was six or seven and we began to look at his baby pictures — we decided either I had a very bad camera or he was just average.

Maybe even between average and ugly to tell the truth —
like minus three on a scale of one-to-ten. But where the
funny part comes in is that he has a son Robert the Third.
and his grandmother, Peg, says "Robert the III is just beautiful, and he looks just like Bob did when he was a baby."
    Images tend to get mixed up in people's minds and that's
one reason I think I like that phrase —
        "...*to share in the very being of God.*"

            I believe that really I would rather
                    be like God
                than to look like God.
And I think I'd like it even more if I could really decide all
that was meant by "the very being of God."
    I'm a quiet speaker, in fact, those behind the fourth row
usually say I'm *really* a quiet speaker. I like to tease and say
that I was taught in seminary that if you didn't have anything
to say...say it loud. But there's something about me though,
that the more important something seems to be to me
                the quieter I say it
            and if it's really sacred to me
                I'll probably whisper.
And when I speak I stand still, usually with one hand in my
pocket, and I'm just not the kind of guy that looks excited.
I wish I could wave my arms and beat on the desk and things
like that that would let folk know I am really excited, but at
my age, I might hurt myself.

            And if I were talking to you now
            you would probably have to lean
                    forward in your chair
                to hear me — but inside
        when I think of "sharing the very being of God,"
            I am almost jumping up and down.

        And so I want to write to you about some things
                that are filling me
                and touching me

and blessing me
and warming me
and changing me
and causing me to wonder what I really
might be if I could learn to "share in His very being."

CHAPTER III

CHAPTER III

Not Even Sick

You see a lot of funny bumper stickers these days, like the one on the back of the big truck, "If you can't stop, smile as you go under." I'm not sure about the one that says, "Your God may be dead but mine is alive and well." Now I think you believe that, don't you, the "God is dead" crowd seems to be dying out, but I sometimes believe that we fail to act as if God is life and that to share in this being is to share in His life.

Last fall, I was speaking on a college campus for opening week, and I was supposed to have a rap session each night in a different dorm. They were supposed to ask the questions and I was supposed to give the answers. Well, I thought I'd be in over my head pretty fast, so I decided it would be good to sing a lot together. With luck we could sing right through the questions and answers. We were singing "God Is So Good" and I said I know three or four verses and it only takes four syllables, so why don't we just write some verses and let's just keep it going.

I really did it also because they were singing very beautifully and we sang,

"He Is My Lord,"
"I Love Him So,"
"Coming Again,"
"He Answers Prayer"

and finally somebody led us in

> **"God is not dead**
> **God is not dead**
> **God is not dead**
> **He's so good to me."**

Do you know what I wanted to sing for the next verse — and
did — and they thought I was kidding, but I really meant it.

> **"Not even sick**
> **Not even sick**
> **Not even sick**
> **He's so good to me."**

I not only believe God is alive — I don't even think He's sick.

They say that as you get older there is less and less room
in your medicine chest. And Peg and I, for varying reasons
and ailments, take an assortment of pills each night.
Generally the last thing we do at night before we go to bed
is to meet at the sink for our nightly ritual of pill rolling.
Now she has some big ones that are prettier than mine, but
I take more than she does so I think it about evens out.
The other night, just for fun, I said,

> "Let's take all the pills we have in the house
> and line them up and close our eyes
> and have mystery pill time
> and we'll just bless some unknown organ in our body."

I know this is not an earth-shaking statement but somehow
it means a lot to me.

> I don't think God takes pills for headaches
> or tranquilizers because He can't cope.
> And I meant it when I sang

"Not even sick."
He is alive and well and at work in His world.

Now I'm fairly sure that we all believe that but if you really want to practicalize a little, we don't act very much like we believe it. In fact, we act like He's sort of sickly and we had better take good care of Him.

It's almost like we've put Him in a jar and keep Him down at the front of the church and we say,

"Do you want to come down and see God?"

Oh, of course, we'll punch some holes in the lid so He can get some air, but not big enough holes so He can get out. And the people come down and they say — yeah — take the lid off, let me see Him. Oh, no, if we did that, He might get out there in the world He created and get stomped or trampled. We'd better keep Him in the jar here on the altar. I secretly suspect that He'll be alright and that He is out there at work in a thousand ways we never suspect.

In the King James Version in the Prologue to John's gospel, there is a phrase that says,

"Without Him was not anything made that was made."

But here again I like the New English Bible translation because it seems so much more positive. It simply says,

"All that came to be was alive with His life."

But we all have trouble looking at all of life like it came from Him. We have this way of categorizing everything — "it's us over here" with God's life and then it's just them "over there." It's like we're the good guys and they are the bad guys, like we have on the white hats and they have on the black hats. (I can just imagine myself in a big white hat— about a ten-gallon hat on a two-quart head.)

And we say,
"We're the ones,
we're the church,
we're the good guys with the white hats
and God's over here with us"

And then — they're the bad guys and everybody knows God

doesn't have anything to do with the bad guys. Why can't we see that "all that came to be was alive with His life" and that God's out there just working away with the good guys and the bad guys — the good guys who want to be good and the good guys who want to be bad and the bad guys who want to be bad and the bad guys who want to be good

and all the in-betweens.

In fact, when Christ was on earth, the big problem to the White Hat Society was that they couldn't keep him away from the bad guys. He just wouldn't put on the white hat and stay where He belonged. He was always out there with those bad guys —

just like He loved them
and cared for them
and wanted to eat supper with them.

I was up for a kind of a three day vacation with Peg a couple of years ago and we were out on Nantucket which is about thirty miles off the coast of Cape Cod. My wife is a shopper, she *is* a shopper, and I am not a shopper but she likes to shop and since we were on vacation in the interest of fellowship and harmony we were shopping. And they had a lot of souvenir shops which we went through in a hurry. It had once been the whaling capital of the world and they had everything in the shape of a whale.

Ash trays, posters, wall-plaques, glasses,
jars, bottles, watches, charms, bracelets,

whatever you needed they had one in the shape of a whale plainly marked

SOUVENIR OF NANTUCKET
on the front and
MADE IN JAPAN
on the back.

But there was one lovely place we went — a gift shop called the Cross-Eyed Dove. And when we walked in, we knew this was not just a souvenir shop. Whoever owned this shop had bought and displayed everything with care and love. Somebody who liked nice things. In the pottery and sculptures, and paintings and macrames, there were

textures and
shapes
colors and sizes
and beauty.

And you instantly knew that here was someone who had taste and love for beauty. Fortunately for me everything there wasn't Peggy's taste.

The owner's name was Robin and we became acquainted with her. She had worked around the corner in the "whale store" when the opportunity had presented itself to open her own shop. She told her previous employers that she was going to fill her shop with things she loved. And they told her that she would starve to death. Buy the things you like and put them in your house. But for the store buy all the silly, dumb things that the tourists will buy and sell to them and then go home to the things you love. But that wasn't what Robin wanted to do and she didn't.

On our last day there we were waiting on the ferry and Robin came along from lunch. And we were visiting for the last time.

"Tell me again what you do," she said.
I'm in the religious publishing business."
"I don't believe much in religion."
"Is that right?"
"Yes, I don't think I believe in God."
"Well, I think you do."
"No, I don't."
"But I think you do."
"Well, why do you say that?"

"Well, maybe you don't know and believe in God in a personal sense, but you like so many of the things He does. You know all the colors and shapes and textures and fibers and wood and clay—all the things you love come from His hand for all that came to be is alive with His life. And you may not call on His name yet, but you'd really like Him

because you already like so many things about Him."
We were back up there the next summer and were going
up the street to her shop when we met her. "Do you
remember us?" "Sure, you're the Bensons, and you're the
one who tried to convert me." "No, I was the one that was
trying to tell you you were already partly converted."

Am I trying to say to you that Robin could accept Christ
because she likes pottery, or that there is another way to the
Father except through Christ? No, I know about redemption
and forgiveness and the cross and the blood and confession
and profession. But are you trying to say to me that God is
not alive and speaking to Robin in a hundred different ways?

The jar is just too small.

In my Sunday School class I like to ask trick questions —
questions when I know the only answer and everyone else's
is wrong. That's my favorite kind of question because I look
so intelligent when I come out with the answer. Being college
kids, one of them usually is a step or two ahead of me and
aces me out. One of my best efforts in this category of
questions was "What are some of the gospel songs used in
the last five or ten years that you think have really been a
blessing?" And they answered,

"He Touched Me"
"Fill My Cup"
"How Great Thou Art"

They never seem to name any songs we publish. Then very
quietly and profoundly I say, "Why didn't anyone say, 'He
Ain't Heavy, He's My Brother'?"

"That's not a gospel song!" You mean it is not gospel to
say that you love your brother so much that when you have
to carry him, you don't even notice his weight, and that you
love him so much you're never, never embarrassed because
he's a cripple? Are you saying that's not what Christ was
talking about?

I'm not saying we ought to include it in the new hymnal
or even sing it next Sunday morning in the service. But when
the answer is — that's not a gospel song because one of us

white hats didn't write it, that was written by one of the bad guys — I always think of the verse,

"all that came to be was alive with His life."

I think God is alive in His world and I wonder how many times He wants to talk to us and how much He wants to show us and how much He'd teach us in a day's time if we believed that He was as alive on Monday as He is on Sunday. I want to see what He's doing and hear what He has to say. And one of the things I want to say in this book is that if we come to "share in the very being of God" we are going to begin to sense about Him that He is Life and that His life is everywhere. It is in the music and the heartbeat and the pulse and throb of the world He made.

Last fall, I was going to plant a tulip and iris bed under some trees along the side of our yard. Tom, my ten-year-old, and I went over in a creek bed and got some stones and we had our trailer loaded with those stones and peat moss and dirt and, pardon the expression, sheep manure and the shovels, and hoes, and iris bulbs. And we got started and when we quit for the day, the trailer was loaded with a mixture of all the junk and dirt and plastic bags.

The next weekend it turned cold and I know you won't believe this, but I didn't ever get back to finish the job. A month or so later my brother came over to borrow the trailer, and he did just what I would have done if I had borrowed his — he just raked the whole mess right out on the hillside — rakes, hoes, towsacks, plastic bags, bulbs — and took the trailer. The winter came and I never did get back up there.

But sometime in the dead of winter — maybe on a cold, grey day — God slipped up there and whispered to those bulbs,

"He forgot you, didn't he?
That's the way with old Bob,
he starts a lot of stuff he just doesn't finish;
he means well, but he just left you
laying there in all that trash;

but don't you worry,
because I have put within you life.
You are filled with My life."

I was up there on the hill the other day to see if my brother
had returned the trailer and if the tractor would start. He
had and it wouldn't. It was one of the first warm days of
spring and right there in all that junk do you know what
was happening? Those iris were just growing away. Life,
indefinable, indescribable life — the life of God in an iris bulb.

I'm whispering now —
I'm talking about sharing
the being of God
and God is life and we are to share that life and
He will touch us and bless us with that life.

I was trying to think how one might describe life
so that I would make "the life of God"
stand out in your mind and one of the things
you say about life is that it grows.

But you don't hardly want to say
that God is growing.
It's just better to think of Him
as being the same
yesterday, today
and forever.

In my Sunday School class we were talking about this and
Susan said, "No, I can't say He grows — I have to think of
Him as a fixed point in a changing world. Everything else is
moving and rotating and there has to be something or
somebody somewhere that doesn't keep shifting."

Now I agree with that —
there has to be a place where
a person can say, "This is it.
I can count on this."

I see that and I understand that. And yet that's not exactly
what God in His life seems to be to me. Because when you
get this fixed point — always there, stable, unmovable kind
of God — He begins to be like some gigantic telephone pole.

And when you make some kind of misjudgment or miscalcu-
lation you just run headlong into Him and go crashing
through the windshield of your life. And when I look at it
like that, it doesn't help me as much.

I think I am beginning to believe that the most fixed thing
of all about God
is His very flexibility —
It is His way of showing up at the most unexpected
times and places.

It seems that part of what He was trying to say with His
birth in a manger was precisely this — don't ever be
surprised at where you'll find me — you can look for me
anywhere and anytime and everywhere and all the time.

And there is this flexibility about life — sometimes it takes
awhile, sometimes it moves slow, but it wins. I don't know
who figured the brick for my house, but he way overfigured.
Twelve years later I am still building flower beds and
sidewalks and patios out of those extra bricks. Peggy, the
great shopper, found some lovely old iron rail fence and I
drove up to Lebanon and brought it home and made a
pretty shrubbery and flower bed with the fence and the
bricks out between some trees at the end of our house.
When I made the bed, the bricks were over a foot or so
from the trees, but those crazy trees grew over by my
bricks. And give them another three or four years and
they'll push my wall over. You'd think when you laid a
bunch of heavy bricks around a tree, the tree wouldn't have
a chance.

But it just keeps pushing
and shoving,
it just keeps moving —
it's just alive.

I know you've seen a sidewalk that a tree root has just
picked up. Somebody poured the concrete and said, "Aw,
don't worry about that root — this concrete's heavy." And the
root said, "Aw, don't worry about that concrete — I'm alive,"
and now it's 8 to 2 in favor of the root.

Somehow this year in our celebration of Easter we wound
up with three rabbits and two ducks. This involved the
building of an apartment complex for ducks and rabbits.
As long as they were in boxes in the storage room and we
took them out to play with them, they were fairly tame...
but when we moved them out into the hutch-cage, or cage-
hutch, and they got bigger, they got harder to catch. And
you had to slip one hand in the cage and say, "Here,
ducky, ducky," while you gently slipped your other hand
in the other corner for them to run into.

And one of the things about the very being of God
is that it moves and loves and cares
and gently pushes its way
into every corner of your life.

I believe in the fixed point theory, but I also believe in the
life of God, that is flexible and is "in everything that came to be."
The other afternoon I was holding devotions at a
retirement home. And I was really believing this thing about
life and the fact that it ought to be exciting and new and
different and if God lives in your life there should be an
alertness and an awareness. But on the way over, I was
thinking to myself, "It's one thing for you to say those
things because you are up and about

and you take trips
and you're well and happy
and you like your job
and you have a nice family and friends
with whom you can share
and you're not stuck away in a rest home.

Sure — you can say it is great and exciting to be alive and
have God's life, but do you have any right to say it to those
people. At the ripe old age of forty-three, could I honestly
say this to people who were sixty-three and seventy-three
and eighty-three, and maybe even more. And so I frankly
confessed to them, "Maybe you should be talking to me
because I have never been where you are and all of you
have known and experienced the things that I am going

through. You've raised your kids and built your businesses and lived a great portion of your lives. Really, you should be telling me, but I've been invited here to speak, so I guess I'll talk to you.

"However, if at the end you disagree, I'd like for you to tell me about it. If there really is a cutoff point where God's life no longer means what I am trying to say it should mean to you, then I honestly want you to tell me about it. If what I'm saying is just for teenagers, or young adults, or middle-agers or if it stops at 55 or when you retire, or 72 or 87½, I ought to know this. Because to believe in the life of God for myself, I also have to believe in it for you, even though some of you are 30 and 40 years older than I am. So if I'm wrong, I want you to come and tell me — I honestly do."

About halfway back on the left hand side there was a very distinguished lady sitting whom I judged to have been somewhere in her seventies. As you probably can imagine, I am a very, very witty speaker and writer. In fact, some people have told me that I should be a comedian. Lots of people have told me I should be doing *something* different. But she didn't even smile. And then I know you have noticed how inspirational I am and how I can just touch and move you to tears. Well, she didn't cry either.

To be real honest, her only response that I noticed was a yawn and then I don't know what else she did after that, because I don't look at people who yawn while I am speaking, since I know how embarrassing it is for the speaker to be looking at me when I yawn. But afterward she came up and stood off to one side while I visited with some of the other people. You know how people say, "That was a good talk, Sonny." And when the rest of the people had moved along she took my hand and told me her name and said to me,

"I just want you to know
that every morning when I open my eyes,
before I ever take my head off the pillow,
whether it's sunny or rainy,
I thank God for the day,
for every day is a bonus."

Now that thrilled me because I want to be her age someday
and I want to look at every day as an "extra" portion of the
life of God for me.

Martin Buber, in his book, *Meetings*, tells of being the
guest "of a noble old thinker" with whom he had once
spoken at a conference. "At that time, I was happily
surprised at how the man with steel-grey locks asked us at
the beginning of his talk to forget all that we believed we
knew about his philosophy from his books. In the last years,
which had been war years, reality had been brought so close
to him that he saw everything with new eyes and had to
think in a new way. Buber concludes:

> *"To be old is a glorious thing*
> *when one has not unlearned*
> *what it means to begin;*
> *this old man had even perhaps*
> *first learned it thoroughly in old age.*
> *He was not at all young*
> *but he was old in a young way,*
> *knowing how to begin,"*

Let me brag a little —
I have a grandson named Robert Green Benson, III.
Now, in case you're not big on family trees
   that makes me Robert Green Benson, Sr.
And I have a son Robert Green Benson, Jr.
   and a grandson Robert Green Benson, III.

Before he was born we were duly notified
   that in the event the baby was a boy, he would be so named
      and we were to call him Robert.
Peering across the gap between the generations
   I took this to mean that we were not to make the same
      mistake of re-using such terms as
   Bobby or little Bobby or Baby Bobby —
   it was to be Robert.
It seemed like quite a handle to me
        for less than ten pounds of humanity —
it seemed very awkward to say, "Goochy-goochy" Robert.

But Robert it was —
        until somebody started calling him "Pookie"
        or just "Pook" for short.
Now Bobby sounds better to me than Pookie
                but then what do grandfathers know?

But a little while after Robert was born
        Tom, my ten-year-old, said to his mom,
"Robert sure is lucky."
                        And Peg wanted to know why
                        Robert was so lucky in Tom's mind.
"Because he gets to do all them new things."
                        And now she wanted to know what all
                        those new things were that Tom
                        was referring to.
"Well," Tom began,
        "He's never climbed a tree
            or waded in the lake
                or run through a field
                    or felt the wind in his face
                        or ridden a bicycle —
                        ALL THEM NEW THINGS."

And I was thinking later about all of God's children
            and about our life in the Spirit
        and about all the wonderful surprises
        and stupendous things He has for all of us to do
                        and see
                    and feel
                        and be
and how we just sit down where we came in
        and how we have all the questions
            and all the answers
    and know all the things to say and sing
        and how we know all the steps and plans
for everybody else and their children, too.
            About how we rigidize and dilute
            and I wonder how many new joys
                        and insights
            and ways of punching holes in the darkness

and poems
and songs and smiles
and simple pleasures we miss
because we cannot begin to conceive how lucky we are,
because in Him there are "all them new things."

CHAPTER IV

CHAPTER IV

All Them New Things

Maybe it is not so strange that we have such difficulty in believing that the world is filled with His life. There is ample evidence about to support the cruelty and injustice of the world in which we live. There is an old Yiddish proverb that says "If God lived on earth people would break his windows."

But the fact that we also treat God as if He were a wheelchair patient in the church is utterly surprising. For instance, some people feel that God must be carefully protected and explained or He will not have enough life to make himself heard through His Word.

I am somewhere between amused and irked at all the people who feel that only through their eternal vigilance will God be able to speak through the Bible. If they are not careful, some group of translators will silence God forever.

Recently in Nashville a group of minister-marchers protested against the new paraphrase of the Scriptures called The Living Bible. The polite name for them is "ultra-conservative," a term which can also be roughly translated "red neck." Now you generally protest in Nashville in one of two places — the State Capitol or the Baptist Book Store. Since there were no Living Bibles on sale at the Capitol the logical place seemed to be the Baptist Book Store and so they came, and so they marched.

Now, I don't doubt for an instant the sincerity of what they were trying to do, but I am convinced just as surely that if nobody ever goes down on Broad Street at the corner of Tenth across from the old Union Station and marches in front of the Baptist Book Store, God is and will be speaking to people through His Word. No group of translators or scholars can lock God out of His own Word. He is alive and He speaks through His book.

This is a God-book. I certainly believe that as earlier and earlier manuscripts are found, men should carefully and diligently study and through deep research make every attempt to discover as nearly as possible the exact things that God was saying through these men who wrote the Holy Bible.

But this is the God-book.
   It is the speaking word of God
      and His ability to speak through it
    does not depend on minister-marchers
 or involved hassles between various groups of
   fundamentalists
    on tenses and Greek and Hebrew words
or English words whose meanings have changed through
  history.
It is the living, healing,
    moving, probing, convicting, speaking Word —
it is the God-book and
    He has been
   and He is
  and He always will be heard through it.
For it is filled with His life —
  it is the Living Word of God.

My Dad used to have a funny saying when I first went to work with him. I was young and energetic and just wanted to change everything because I was bubbling over with new ideas to try. And he used to relate to me a story about one of his customers, an old gentleman, who ran a private summer camp for boys. Dad printed the catalog and every year the owner's young daughter wanted to completely redo the book. Finally one year in exasperation, he told his daughter, "The purpose of the catalog is to recruit campers and we have had a full enrollment for the past ten years. This catalog is doing its job. If you want to doctor something — go find something that is sick." And my Dad, who was running a successful business without me, reminded me more than once that if I had to change something — find something that was sick.

And I would say to you, if you want to march or protest or hassle, find something that is sick — the Bible is the living Word of God and He is speaking through it. It is the God-book.

It is a God-book, but I am also convinced that his life makes it a "me book" also. Out on the West Coast there is a company that has devised a very ingenious scheme for personalizing children's books. I'm sure the color illustrations throughout the book are printed in large mass runs for economy's sake. Then on the basis of information the buyer sends along with the order, each book is run through a computer. Such questions as the child's name, age, birthday, street address, friends and dog or cat's name and other assorted tidbits like sock size are put on the order blank. When the book is printed by the computer, each book is a story with the child as the chief character.

Last Christmas my mother had one of these books for our youngest son, Patrick. You can hardly imagine his surprise and delight when he pulled it out from under the tree and unwrapped it and began to read:

> *"Once upon a time in a place called Hendersonville,*
> *there lived a little boy named Patrick Benson.*
> *Now Patrick wasn't just an ordinary little boy.*
> *This is a story about one of his adventures.*
> *It's the story of the day that Patrick met a giraffe."*

Over seventy times Patrick and his street and his friends were named and when he got better acquainted with the

giraffe it even had the same birthday and its name was
"Kcirtap," which if you didn't notice is Patrick spelled
backwards.

Do you think Patrick likes that book? It is one of his
favorite and most important books because to him it is a
"me-book."

I'm sure you all have read *Winnie-the-Pooh*. If you
haven't your education is not complete. It is a delightful
story for children that is even more fun for adults.
A. A. Milne wrote the stories or told them first to his son,
Christopher Robin. It begins with Christopher Robin coming
down with his stuffed bear.

> *Here is Edward Bear, coming downstairs now,*
> *bump, bump, bump, on the back of his head*
> *behind Christopher Robin. It is, as far as he*
> *knows, the only way of coming downstairs, but*
> *sometimes he feels that there really must be*
> *another way, if only he could stop bumping and*
> *think of it. And then he feels that perhaps there*
> *isn't. Anyway, here he is at the bottom, and*
> *ready to be introduced to you. Winnie-the-Pooh.*
> *…"What about a story?" said Christopher*
> *Robin. "What about a story," I said. "Could*
> *you very sweetly tell Winnie-the-Pooh one?"*
> *"I suppose I could," I said, "What kind of*
> *stories does he like?" "About himself. Because*
> *he's that sort of a bear."*

And I suspect we are all *that* sort of bears. We like stories
about ourselves. And this living book of God is about us.
Read it, the King James, the Revised Standard Version, the
New English Bible, the Living Bible, in the Greek and Hebrew
or any one of a dozen other translations and you will find that
He will be saying things to you

that guide

and comfort

and bless and heal

and answer

the deep questions of your life.

We are in that book — it is a "me-book" and a "you-book."
We all have taken our turn at saying, "There is no room in
this inn," and we all know what it is like to sadly reverse our
paths like the rich, young ruler. And we all know what it is
to say, "I do not know Him," or to leave unsaid, "Yes, I am
a follower of His." We all have bravely said in stirring faith,
"Thou art the Christ, the Son of the Living God," and we all
have felt or said, "Unless I touch the prints of His hands."

It is not just a book written a long time ago about some
people who lived way back then. It is about us. It is not just
a book about a few men to whom He said, "Lo, I will never
leave you," it is to us as well these words still speak. It was
not only their sorrow He promised to "turn into joy" but He
was saying to us just as surely as if He were looking us in the
face that the thing that seems like sorrow to us today, He would
have us writing poems and singing songs about tomorrow
or next week. These things were said to us and for us and
about us in this living book of God.

Now, we all believe that, don't we? I haven't written anything that we wouldn't all nod our heads in agreement on,
have I? Then why don't or why can't we act like this is the
living word. Why do we say I try to read the Bible, but it just
is dull, monotonous, and routine. Maybe it is because we
haven't realized that it is a "me-book" and that He was not
only speaking to Paul on the Damascus Road, but He was
just as surely speaking to Patrick on Bayshore Drive.

We should be able to hear God
smiling and breathing,
and whispering
and shouting and laughing
and crying to us
in His word.

Sometimes a part of the problem is that we get confused on
the matter of "rightly dividing the word of truth." I don't
understand all I know about that phrase, but it generally
means that we take the good parts, like "Blessed is the man"
and say that means me, and the sticky, knotty parts about
denial and failure and sacrifice and feel that means the
other fellow.

Nothing, I guess, is more discouraging to a minister than to come to a service with the truth of God laid deeply on his heart and with every fiber of his being deliver that message only to have someone say afterward, "That sure was good, preacher. It's just a shame *they* weren't here to hear it."

Reuben Welch in his book, *We Really Do Need Each Other,* makes this point very strongly in writing about the first chapter of First John:

> *"I don't think it is right*
> *that there should be*
> *any part of the Bible*
> *about which we can say.*
> *Oh, I've already finished that exercise —*
> *now let's go on to something else.*
> *I've passed my exam on First John.*
> *I have a feeling that all of the Bible*
> *keeps speaking to all of us*
> *all of the time*
> *and...this passage has something*
> *to say to us*
> *wherever we are on our spiritual journey."*

I think it would be interesting now if you would take your scissors and just trim out of your Bible all the passages that you feel don't apply to you any more, because you feel you have already attained them. That way you could find the things you need so much quicker. It would be a much better system than marking your Bible, because then you wouldn't have to read through all those verses that were obviously written for "them."

I think in our stripped-down personalized edition we could start out with deleting the story about Nicodemus. No need to keep reading that because it is very obviously written to people who need to be "born again."

One of my best friends was preaching on this passage the other day and his two main points were repentance and obedience, neither of which happens to be mentioned in this story and I asked him where he got all that fine truth he was putting on us. And we had a good laugh about it.

But the story is about being born again, so we don't really
need to read it, because we have already been born again.
It's for "them."
        Unless, just possibly
    there was some faint chance
        He was saying to me and you
    that we need to be born again
            and again
        and again
            and again
        and again.

Now, I know a little theology. I know that we equate the
terms like "being born again" with "getting saved" or
"professing Christ" and others and I am not trying to indicate
that we need to get saved at every revival meeting and a
couple of times in between. I am sure though that I don't
want anybody to take away my God-given right to backslide.
In our church, and probably yours also, we believe in it and
practice it.

Jesus was trying to explain to Nicodemus the difference
between rules, deeds, codes, conduct and a genuine life in
the Spirit.
    Nicodemus was puzzled by
        Jesus' choice of words.
        How can I enter my mother's womb again?
    And I believe Jesus sat there
    with Nicodemus on a wall or a curb
    and said, "Well, it's like...oh —
            how can I make you see..."
        and about that time
        a breeze came blowing across the field
    and down the street and leaped
            upon the wall or curb beside them
        and tugged at their beards
        and rustled their robes
                and Jesus said,
    "That's the way it is, Nicodemus.
        Where did the wind come from?"
                "I don't know."

"And where's it going?"
"I don't know."
"Well, that's the way it is with the Spirit,
            it's that way with the life of God.
It's like the breeze—
                  it blows across your life
         and you don't know where it came from
            or where it is going
               or where it will take you.
   You only know you're different,
      you only know you're better—
            that your life is changed
                  and cleaned and blessed.
   You only know your life means more
      than it ever did before.
            You must be born again."

There is an old illustration that has been used by preachers and ministers so long that no one really remembers the town or the man's name correctly. But the truth is there. You have probably heard it; it is about the town drunk who was converted at every revival meeting. And the men on the square and in the barber shop would always laugh and say, "But it won't last." In a book called *Love Is Something You Do*, Frederick Speakman tells the story and concludes:

"They always clubbed old Governor Campbell
back into the gutter with that statement
'It won't last!'
Of course it won't last! Who cares?
Who cares, if for a while it makes
a real difference,
if it can see you through until your heart
can be caught again on the surge
of another of God's incoming tide.

'That's the trouble with religion,'
they used to say, and
the barber would look up and listen
as if to hear some final word on the matter.

*'You take old Governor Campbell —
why he gets converted at every revival.'
But all the while the tragedy was
that he wasn't converted often enough.*

Can you remember the day you fully realized the warmth
of God's forgiving love and the eagerness with which you
sought His way with every part of your being? Do you still
recall the newness which surrounded your life when He
transformed you? Is there still a tremor of excitement as you
live again the moment when "life more abundant" began to
flood all that was you? Then can you believe that was
supposed to be a once-in-a-lifetime happening and that now
by striving and by discipline and testifying of those good old
days, you are to somehow recall and retain the warmth and
wonder of those first days?

When I think of it like that I'm not sure but what this
passage maybe ought not to be snipped out of our Bibles,
but that maybe we ought to read it and believe it has something to say to us right now. The spiritual life has its very
existence in a series of new births. There must always be new
growth, new buds, new adventures if our spiritual self is
to continue to be.

Someone is always saying Jesus said, "So and so," in such
a way as to make you believe that's all He ever said and that
He said it to everybody He ever met. I don't know why, but
in a perverse sort of way, I would like to make a thorough
study and catalogue everything He said to everybody. I'd
file it by subject and by the person to whom He said it.

And then, when one of those one-and-only-one-answer
people said, "Yes, but Jesus told so and so that he should
do so and so," I would be able to say that's true. He did say
that. There are seventy-eight, or whatever number it turned
out to be, recorded conversations with individuals and He
said what you mentioned to three of them. The other
seventy-five He told something else.

One of my nobler reasons for wanting to do this is to see
and maybe help others to see that Jesus in His life and in
His Word didn't have a memorized speech or a check list

of things to say. He came to be a channel through which the life of God flowed and it rushed into men exactly at the point of their need — always.

And the Word of God, this living book reveals the very life of God to each of us at precisely the point to which we need to be spoken.

I am saying if we find meaning
in the phrase
"sharing in the very being of God,"
first of all, we will be sharing
in the life of God —
in everything He made,
which is everything that is,
and in His Word.
I don't know where you are on your journey,
I don't know where you've been or
the rut out of which He lifted you.
I can only imagine it has been very
exciting for His life to flow through you.
But I am also convinced that
there are blessings
and joys and graces
and bits of truth and
gentle guidance —
there are whispers from His voice
and occasional glimpses of His being
that will make "life more abundant,"
a phrase that never ceases
to have new and deeper
meaning for you.

CHAPTER V

CHAPTER V

Beyond Retrieval

I have been trying to say to you that at least a part of what "sharing in the being of God" must mean is to share in the life of God. As I am writing this morning, I can hear the birds singing and at breakfast I saw the squirrels playing in the yard. My mother called on the phone and invited Patrick and Tom to go to the circus this afternoon with all their cousins, and they are as alive with excitement and joy as only eight and ten-year-olds can be. Mike is home from college and is bigger than I am now and we have been wrestling in the den. I am not strong enough to beat him and he is too polite to whip me, so we just struggle and groan until I can't go any farther and then we just lay there exhausted, laughing and panting for breath in a heap. Mostly he laughs and I pant for breath. Out by the porch a pair of cardinals is building a new nest in the cherry laurel bush, because a blue jay found the old one and killed all their babies. On my three acres this morning there is life.

Yes, I've read the headlines and I saw the news on TV last night about death and murder and wickedness in high places and in low. But nothing I saw or heard or read even remotely altered my belief that God is involved with man. First He creates, He breathes into us and into our world life. Secondly, these things did not keep me from believing, maybe even more strongly than ever, that He cares.

And it is this second theme that I would like to think about with you now. He cares; God is love. One would have to know very little about "the very being of God" if he did not realize that God is a compassionate, caring being.

I guess the place to start when you think of the love of God is Jesus. He said, "He who has seen me has seen the Father." In other words, the Father is like what I am like.

In our Sunday School class we generally study one of the Gospels, the most recent being the Gospel of John. We take a very leisurely journey through the book and on occasion have taken as long as a year and a half to make it all the way through. Now this is certainly not because of my brilliance as a Bible scholar, but it is a class of college students and they go and come and I also have to be away from time to time. In fact, the other day they were taking a survey of the Sunday School with the idea of going to double sessions in the fall. One of my class members made a comment in response to the question, what could we do to improve the class, that blessed me some but not altogether. The answer was, "Have Bob Benson there more often."

But the longer we spend in the gospels the more I am impressed that if the Father is indeed like Jesus, then God is love. That Jesus came at all is hard to comprehend and can only be explained in terms of love.

            The headlines are shocking —
                not necessarily for the
            things that nations do,
                    for national deeds look respectable
                        enough carried out beneath
                the polished surfaces of diplomacy —
            but for the things that
                        men do to men — individually —
                    in anger, in passion, in greed
                        in sheer frustration and for

absolutely meaningless motives —
the atrocities, the assaults,
the meanness, the wickedness
the dark deeds of men.

To think of grown men attacking
little girls and groups of young adults
taking the lives of people
they never knew or saw before
for reasons that do not have
even a vague validity
makes me shudder at the depth
to which we sink.
In fact, it makes us hesitate
to use the word *we* at all —
couldn't we somehow disown
or read out of the family of men
all these who bring us such shame —
couldn't we shut them out
like "black sheep" or distant cousins —
must they come to our family reunions?

Do we have to admit the fact that
we ever went to school with them
or that they once had dreams and hopes
that were strangely like our own?

And to think that He came
and made Himself a member
of a family that had sons and daughters
that rob and cheat
and blunder and murder
and steal from one another
and that He steadfastly believed
there was good in all of us
and resolutely maintained that
He had come to see that somehow
it would come to the surface
in each one of us.
This really is hard to comprehend.

At some point, I'm not sure when or where, Jesus must have decided that the best and most powerful manner in which He could accomplish that which He had come to do — was to just care. With all the power and strength of angels and creation within the realm of His being as the Son of God, He chose and committed Himself as the Son of Man to simply and purely love people. And I believe He chose that way because He knew it was the most effective thing that He could do. And he went out and did just that.

I had a lady in my church up in Modesto, California, who was an old lady. She lived on what must be the longest street in California — it's called Frontage Road. She was a Senior, Senior Citizen. But she was sturdy and alert and although she had had a hard life she had met it head on and still was remarkably independent and just "fiesty." She liked to argue with me, her learned pastor fresh from seminary, about the scriptures. The church was small and I only had a few people to visit and went to see her fairly often. I don't mind arguing a little myself from time to time.

So I'd go to see her and one of our favorite topics for these intense discussions was Judas. I don't know why she liked to argue about Judas so much, but I think one of her favorite verses in the whole Bible was the one that said, "Judas was a devil from the beginning." I don't know why that verse gave her such hope and consolation and assurance. It just seemed to be a blessed truth to her that he was "a devil from the beginning." I never did really like that verse. I don't have it clipped out of my Bible but I don't have it underlined either. And when I'm flipping through and looking for things to bless and touch me, I never hunt up that verse.

I'll tell you the place I like to read about Judas because I think he was within a hair's breadth of being changed by Jesus' love for him. It's over in John's gospel at the last supper and Jesus was saying in deep agitation of spirit, "In truth I tell you one of you is going to betray me." And the disciples looked at one another in bewilderment. "Who could he be talking about." And one of them, "the disciple whom Jesus loved," a humble term that John used to describe himself, was sitting by Jesus and Simon Peter leaned over and whispered, "Ask Him who He means." And John, as he reclined, leaned over toward Jesus and just as cool as he could, like it really wasn't a big deal or anything like that, said, "Who is it?" You know you have to be calm in situations like that when you're asking a question you're dying to know the answer to and yet you want to look like you are just mildly interested.

Jesus said, "It's the man to whom I give this piece of bread after I have dipped it in the dish." So it must have been fairly obvious when he handed the bread to Judas. Then he said to Judas, "Whatever you feel you must do, go ahead now and do it."

Now, here's the interesting part to me. Here was this small group of thirteen people eating supper in a small room and Jesus spoke to Judas in such a quiet tone that when he left the room the next verse says that no one else at the table knew why he left or what Jesus meant. They supposed he had gone to pay for the meal or make some arrangements about giving to the poor.

Jesus, in the last hours before His deepest agony and travail, within hours of an excruciating death was still making quiet, kindly entreaties to his betrayer. If it had been you or me, we would probably have said to the others, "There he is, the dirty fink, after all I've done for him. He's the one. He's headed out right now to finish the deed. He never has really understood or really been one of us. But just before he goes I want the other eleven of you to look at Him. I want you to see what a betrayer looks like — we ought to shave his head or something. See him, low down betrayer. He's the one. You can leave now, go on, beat it."

But quietly he said, "If you must, if you're in so deep, you can't turn back — go ahead and don't prolong your suffering." And with that dear old lady's precious promise, notwithstanding to the contrary, I believe with all my heart if Judas had said, "It's too late to stop it now, but I am so sorry and miserable — would you forgive me?" there would be a story in the gospel about a Judas whose life would have been different because Jesus loved and cared right to the end. I believe that if Judas

had come to the cross the next day when Christ was so nearly
dead, He couldn't have spoken. His eyes would have said to
Judas, "It is okay, you are forgiven," and that look of love
would have changed the life of Judas forever.

Jesus chose the power of love and believed in its ability
to change the hearts of men.

Isn't it strange that we should glorify the cross,
     put it on our churches
   wear it on our lapels
        and around our necks —
   that we should sing about it
    and that it should become
  a symbol of faith and inspiration —
      the cross — a dark, dirty excruciating
  way of legalized killing
    in the name of justice.

Had the Romans chosen to hang
    or behead, or mutilate or shoot
  would we sing of the precious old rope
or would our steeples lift rifles to the sky?
     Isn't it moving that His love
        could transform the long ago counterpart
of electric chairs and gas chambers
into a symbol of faith and devotion.

But then love changes everything it touches
  it makes heavy burdens light,
    long hours short,
      ordinary faces beautiful,
    houses into homes,
   picnics into banquets,
wilted daisies into bouquets,
      God into sacrifice
     and sinners into saints.

And if He could take a cross
    and fashion it like He fashioned wood
   in his earthly father's carpenter shop

> into a depiction of deepest love,
> doesn't it make you wonder
> what He might be able to do with you
> if you yielded to His love?

When I talk about this nearly always somebody comes up and says to me, "Well, you've got to remember that Jesus got angry, He wasn't always loving and kind. He took a whip and cleaned out the temple." They always want to talk about that and lots of times, although they don't admit it, it is in connection with some problems they are having with their own tempers.

There is always a problem in our thinking about the humanity of Jesus. To quote Reuben Welch's book,*We Really Do Need Each Other,* again:

> *"I think we believe in the humanity of Jesus*
> > *but not really.*
> *I think you think*
> > *you believe in the humanity of Jesus*
> > *but I don't think you really do.*
> > > *And if we would talk about it awhile*
> > > *you'd get nervous."*

There is no problem in saying He was just like one of us. The problem arises when we begin to think — like which *one* of us? And I think it would make you shudder if I wrote or even hinted that Jesus did something He wasn't very proud of — in fact, it would make me shudder, too, and I am not going to write that, or even hint at it.

But I will say if you go through the gospels that never at any other place did He say to anybody, "Well, now, you just better watch out — you do remember that I know how to make whips, don't you, and that I know how to use them — and furthermore, I will if you keep that up?"

And that whip story has never been a great focal point of inspiration in the poetry and hymnody of the church. In fact, there aren't any hymns in our hymnal about it at all. There is such a dearth of materials on this facet of the ministry of Christ, that I started a song about it once:

"Oh, what joy it is to know
when my temper starts to blow
Jesus once got angry, too."

It didn't seem like much of a song and I didn't even finish it.
And I don't think many people would have sung it anyway.

I'm saying I know about the whip and turning over the
tables and I know He used words like "Ye generations of
vipers," but I also know that on His last trip to Jerusalem,
He stopped on the mountainside and looked over the city
and wept because He had wanted to gather it to Himself
and to the Father, even as a mother hen gathers her baby
chickens under her wings.

When I was younger and in Sunday School and youth
meetings, somebody was always coming up with the idea that
it would be good if everyone quoted their favorite scripture
verse. This was generally followed by a loose translation of
John 3:16 and a lengthy silence. Finally someone would
quote that old favorite of us all from John 11:34, "Jesus
wept." I'm sure we all remembered it for its deep truth rather
than for its brevity.

But what a tremendous verse
what a colossal truth —
Jesus wept — He cared
He was touched
He was moved.

And I like to think that weeping, caring, crying is one way
to know a little bit how it feels to be like Jesus and to
share the "very being of God."

Once Jesus was very tired and had taken the disciples
across the Sea of Galilee for a period of rest. He found that
the people had seen them leaving and they had hiked around
the northern edge of the sea and when the boat landed there
were great crowds of people waiting for Him and the scriptures said that even in tiredness and even in the press of
time to be alone with the twelve,

"He looked on the multitude
and was moved with compassion."

Have you ever thought what a beautiful look the look of

compassion really is? The other day Peg and I were on a short trip over to Charleston, South Carolina. We were talking to the stewardess and told her we were changing planes at Washington to go down to Charleston. After a while she came back and said, "Are you talking about Charleston, South Carolina, or Charleston, West Virginia?" We told her that it was South Carolina and then she told us a story of a lady who had been on her flight a few months before. The flight was headed to Charleston, West Virginia, and the lady wanted to go to Charleston, South Carolina. The lady hadn't seen her husband in a year and he was waiting in the airport in South Carolina. She was very, very excited and mentioned South Carolina a time or two and suddenly it dawned on the stewardess what was happening and she had to tell this wife who had waited so long to see her husband that it was still going to be several hours of connecting and waiting before she could see him because somebody had just made a mistake. The stewardess was not exceptionally pretty — really just ordinary looking, but suddenly she was beautiful, for her face was covered with sympathy and caring as she remembered the young wife weeping into Charleston, West Virginia, as her husband waited for a yet to be revealed disappointment in Charleston, South Carolina.

And I am sure the face of Jesus must have shined as He looked at that hungry lonesome crowd. And he preached to them and healed them and took five loaves and two fishes and saw to it that they had their dinners.

What was it that drew men to Jesus? Yes, he spoke with authority and he did deeds of miracle and wonder, but I really think the one thing that men could not ignore was the compassion and love that drained out of His heart and on to His face and words and deeds.

Greek scholars, which is another one of the things that I am not, tell us there are three main words in the Greek language for love. They are "eros," "philos," and "agape."

Eros is a love that is based on desire to have and to own. Anytime someone says I love antiques, or old houses, or modern furniture, or new cars, they usually mean that these are things they would like to have or possess.

Philos is a word that describes a deeper level of love and it connotes friendship or fellowship level. You and I have things in common and there are things I can do for you and things you can do for me and I enjoy being with you and you enjoy being with me.

Both of these loves have one thing in common. Even though they may reach different levels, they have to do with the object of the affection. Erich Fromm writes about this "object-constituted" love in his book, *The Art of Loving.* He says:

> *"Love is not primarily a relationship to a specific person; it is an attitude, and orientation of character which determines the relatedness of a person to the world as a whole, not toward one "object of love." If a person loves only one other person and is indifferent to the rest of his fellow men, his love is not love, but a selfish attachment or an enlarged egotism. Yet, most people believe that love is constituted by the object, not by the faculty. In fact, they even say that it is a proof of the intensity of their love when they do not love anybody but the 'loved' person."*

The other kind of love is the "attitude and orientation of character" love; the Jesus kind of love is called agape and it is love that just loves.

It is a love that doesn't have a set of scales,
   or a yardstick or a ruler,
it doesn't weigh, sift, divide, test,
   examine, qualify, or measure.
It doesn't seek merit or worth
   or beauty, skill or talents.
It doesn't see warts, freckles,
   blemishes or scars.
It doesn't keep ledgers or accounts·
   and there is no periodic printout
     of profit and loss
   and there are no columns
     for debits and credits,

assets and liabilities.
It doesn't talk about inches,
     pounds, cups, miles, quarts;
it just comes in one all-encompassing,
     far-reaching form.
It doesn't have a watch
     or a calendar or a deadline
and does not require a bond
     or a down payment or a credit check.
It doesn't have to be repaid by this Saturday
     or any other for that matter.
And whatever it is you are doing
     when you are judging, qualifying or bargaining,
one thing is for sure — you are not loving,
     not the Jesus kind of loving.
Whenever you say I will "if"
     you have taken a giant step
          away from loving,
     for Jesus loving just says I will,
now, then, in between and all around.
          Love just loves-
     warm, redeeming, forgiving, life-changing
          love.

Jesus' love was love beyond retrieval. We are all very careful, generally, to love in such a way so that if it doesn't turn
out well, we can back away without having lost much pride,
or face. Very cautiously and gently we let our feelings go out,
ready to pull them back on instant notice with a calm look
on our face which says I didn't really care anyway.

But Jesus came and stuck His love so far out there that
there was no way to pick it back up and go nonchalantly on
His way. I know He prayed in the garden in agony that
maybe the cup could pass. And I guess the Father could
have said, "Okay, you tried, you went and they wouldn't
receive you — come on back home and we'll figure out some
other plan." But Jesus had hardly finished the sentence before
He added that He knew it had gone too far — He had cared
too much and shown that love in too many places to pick

it back up now. It was beyond retrieving. It wasn't a case of "picking up the marbles and going home."

As long as you don't say "I care," you're okay because no matter how it turns out you can always say it didn't matter anyway. You can't be hurt because you don't care.

And so you say, "I don't care,"
and someone else says, "I don't care if you don't care,"
"Well, I don't care if you don't care that I don't care."
"So, I don't care if you don't care that I don't care,
if you don't care — so there."

But Jesus said, "I care." If you follow me, I care, if you deny me, I care, if you recognize who I am, I care, if you cannot see yet what I have come to do, I care. Whichever way you go, whatever you do, however it turns out, I care. And you do not go beyond the bounds of His caring — ever, anywhere, at anytime. His was not a "lay it down," "pick it up," "now you see it," "now you don't" kind of love. His love is not based upon your worth or merit; it is based on the steadfast, unchanging quality and attitude of his being, "the very being of God."

Someone came to me the other day
and they were just loaded down
with guilt and hurt and shame.
Tearfully they confessed a wrong
that had long lain dormant.
And what made it even worse was the
confession had only come
after discovery.
The deed and the shame of discovery
before they had confessed themselves
seemed to only double the pain.
There it was now — in the open,
like a giant black spot or smudge
on the pages of their life
and it seemed to cast a cloud
over all the bright, good things
that were really characteristic of them.

And it seemed that we were especially close
    because they were pushed to a real deep
        level in their life
and I, too, was having a chance to reveal how I felt.
    We weren't talking about ball scores or weather,
we were talking about issues that were large
        and deep and real.
I was trying to figure out a way to keep them
from feeling such guilt and shame
and how to believe again in themselves
and most of all in God's forgiveness.

And so I asked them,
    "Do you have any idea how often
    that could happen in your life
    before God gave up on you?"
        "No."
    "Do you know what it would take
    to make Him cease to dream and
    hope for you?"
        "No, I guess I don't."
    "Do you know how many times you would
    have to do that before He even considered
    changing His feelings about you?"
        "No."
"About three times a day for the rest of your life."

There are several places in the gospels where Jesus spoke
of His "hour." One of the places is in John 13:1 where it
says that Jesus knew His "hour" had come, and He must
leave this world and go to be with the Father. No one, I think,
would conclude that Jesus had lived many worthless, useless
hours. Even though there were the long years of preparation,
the things that He accomplished during the days of His
active ministry lead you to believe that the time was spent in
such a way that you would never accuse Him of wasting His
life away. And think of all that was crowded into his earthly
ministry and you are impressed with how He spent His hours.

But He speaks of his "hour" as the one focal hour for
which He had been born. It was the hour for which He had

lived. And the verse explains a bit more about it as it says,
"He had always loved His own who were in the world, and
now He was going to show the full extent of His love."
The finest hour of His life was going to be at the very place
when He showed the deepest point of His love. Not the day
He preached the Sermon on the Mount, not the day He fed
the five thousand, not the times He saved or healed or
blessed, but His "hour," the noblest hour of His life was to
become, as it revealed to the world, the fullest extent of His
love.

So He came to earth in love — love drew Him. He lived in
love and compassion drew Him to the homes of sinners and
to the lepers and demoniacs. And His love drew Him to His
death.

Nearly a year ago Peg and I
had a very hard week.
Wednesday night —
Mike slept downstairs in his room —
where children belong
and we slept upstairs in ours
where moms and dads belong.
Thursday night —
we were 350 miles away and he was
in Ramada 325 and we were in 323 —
connecting rooms and we left the door open
and talked and laughed together.
Friday night —
700 miles from home and
he was in 247 and we were in 239
but it was just down the balcony
and somehow we seemed together.
Saturday night —
he was in the freshman dorm
and we were still in 239.
Sunday night —
we were home and he was
700 miles away in Chapman 309.

Now we have been through this before
Bob Jr. had gone away to college
and we had gathered ourselves together
until we had gotten over it —
mainly because he's married now
and he only lives ten miles away
and comes to visit often
with Deb and Robert the III.
So we thought we knew
how to handle separation pretty well
but we came away so lonely and blue.

Oh our hearts were filled with pride
at a fine young man
and our minds were filled with memories
from tricycles to commencements
but deep down inside somewhere
we just ached with loneliness and pain.

Somebody said you still have three at home —
three fine kids and there is
still plenty of noise —
plenty of ball games to go to —
plenty of responsibilities —
plenty of laughter —
plenty of everything…
except Mike.
And in parental math
five minus one
just doesn't equal plenty.

And I was thinking about God
He sure has plenty of children —
plenty of artists,
plenty of singers,
and carpenters,
and candlestick makers,

and preachers,
plenty of everybody…
except you
and all of them together
can never take your place.
And there will always be
an empty spot in His heart —
and a vacant chair at His table
when you're not home.

And if once in a while
it seems He's crowding you a bit —
try to forgive Him.
It may be one of those nights
when He misses you so much
He can hardly stand it.

This is the Father that Jesus came to reveal and there is
no greater song or hymn than the one you learned early in
Sunday School:

> *Yes, Jesus loves me,*
> *Yes, Jesus loves me,*
> *Yes, Jesus loves me,*
> *The Bible tells me so.*

CHAPTER VI

CHAPTER VI

The Courage To Care

So the "very being of God" must mean love and to share in that being has to mean we are to share in that love for each other. But it is not always easy. In fact, sharing one's real feelings must be one of the hardest things there is to do.

I go to several conventions a year and they all have several things in common. The first is the name badge. Generally about a week before going, I begin to try to train my right eye to look straight ahead at another person's face as I greet them warmly. Then the trick is to train the left eye to wander nonchalantly down to the lapel to find out who in the world it is I am talking to while my right eye keeps them engaged. I generally find their left eye is doing a little homework also. All the time we are talking to each other like long lost friends and calling one another brother to cover up the fact that we don't even remember each other's name.

The second thing begins to evolve out of the natural question, how are you. If it is a group of any one kind of people, like all ministers, or ministers of music, or publishers, or bankers or anything "elses," you begin to hear a couple of words over and over and over.

How are you?
    GR-R-EAT!
And how are you?
    FAN-N-N-TAS-TIC!
How's the work going?
    GR-R-EAT!
How about yours?
    FAN-N-N-TAS-TIC!
And everybody is so great
    and wonderful and super
    and colossal
that you begin to wonder
how anybody could possibly
    have taken time out
for this convention.

And that's just great
    if you're doing great
        and that's fantastic
            if you're really doing fantastic,
but lots of times they are just
    words that shield and hide
because it's not easy to say
    you're just doing lousy
when everybody else is so great.

We do about the same thing at church every Sunday. How're you feeling — but doesn't it bug you when somebody thinks you mean it and they just proceed to tell you how they're feeling from their left ankle all the way up?

It's really a lonely, impersonal world because we are afraid to either admit or listen to true feelings. And yet there are probably more organizations in the United States per square inch than almost anywhere. Will Rogers said, "Americans will join anything in town, why two Americans can hardly meet on the street without banging a gavel and calling the other to order."

I read the other day of 160 people who had a meeting in Staunton, Virginia, and the prize for driving the longest distance went to a couple from Stockton, California. And can you guess what drew all these people from all over the country together for a two-day convention? *They all owned Edsels.*

Seeking, searching for fellowship at almost any level, no matter how superficial it seems to be better than being alone.

Ralph Keyes wrote a very excellent book about the loneliness and lack of community in the United States. In his book, *We The Lonely People,* he says:

> *"Even as we hate being unknown to each other, we crave anonymity. And rather than take paths which might lead us back together, we pursue the very things which cut us off from each other. There are three things which we cherish in particular — mobility, privacy and convenience — which are the very sources of our lack of community."*

He goes on to conclude:

> *"Once the secret's out — that we're all scared — I hope and pray more of us can gather to build communities, and begin by discussing our fear. But to join that community, each one of us must take the hard, terrifying first step — saying to even one person — 'I need you.'"*

And I often wonder how our conventions and assemblies and church gatherings would turn out and how far-reaching their results would be if someone would just have the courage to say:

> "I'm not great —
> I'm not fantastic —
> I'm so discouraged, I'm about to die
> and I need your prayers and love."

And I wonder what would begin to happen if we just began to treat each other like we all had needs and burdens and sensitivities and setbacks. And would we really blow our horn and crowd that poor lady in the green Ford out of the lane if we knew that her children were sick or that her husband had just been laid off?

And I wonder too, how the world would be changed if we didn't think it was a mark of strength and manhood to keep from showing our feelings.

The other day I was riding to a retreat down in Alabama with a couple who picked me up at the airport. And we passed a theatre and Brenda the wife said, "That was the best movie. I cried all the way through it. It was so great, the credits were hardly over before I was crying and I just cried all the way to the very end."

And I said to him, "John, did you cry?"

"Naw," he said.

But she said that the only way he kept from crying was to laugh at her the whole time, especially when he was about to cry himself.

I was reading a little book the other day that was compiled by Marlo Thomas. One of the stories was called "Dudley Pippin and The Principal." It seemed at school that day the sand table had tipped over and the teacher thought Dudley had done it and he was just going home with a very long face after staying after school a long time. He met the principal who said:

"Your teacher must have made a mistake.
It wasn't fair.
We'll do something about it in the morning."
Dudley nodded.
"I bet you'd like to cry," the principal said.
"No," Dudley said, and began to cry.
"Boo-wah, hoo-wah," he cried.
"Booh-hooh, wah-hooh, boo-hoo-wah,"
He cried a long time.
"That's fine," the principal said when Dudley
was through.
"I'm sorry," said Dudley.
"What for?" the principal said,
"You did that very well."
"But only sissies cry," Dudley said.
"A sissy," the principal said,
"is somebody who doesn't cry because
he is afraid someone will call him
a sissy if he does."

Go out to live life, find something that counts and stick your neck out. Spill a little blood, spread some love, shed some tears, it's alright to cry.

We bought an old building and remodeled it for offices and warehouse space. The electrician who did the work was named Richard but he was such a talker that after a while somebody in the building started calling him "Motormouth." He always had a smile and a ready answer to any question, serious or joking. He was a joy to have in the building. In a year or so we were making some additional changes that would require wiring and I asked if anyone had called Richard.

Somebody said, "Didn't you hear about Richard?" "No, I didn't." Well, about two months ago his partner went by the trailer park to go to work with him and Richard said, "I'll just meet you up at the job in about twenty minutes."

And Richard went back into the trailer. He had been arguing with his wife and went back to the bedroom and came back and touched her on the shoulder as she stood at the sink. She turned just in time to see him pull the trigger of the pistol he had pressed against his head.

Richard, "Motormouth," always joking, always laughing, always talking, always willing to be the butt of our jokes was dead. I'd asked him lots of times how he was doing, but I guess I never asked him in such a way that made him want to tell me.

Life in a way is like those electric bump cars at the amusement park. We just run at each other and smile and bump and away we go.

How are you doing —

bump, bump,

Hi, Motormouth —

bump, bump,

Great, fantastic —

bump, bump, bump,

And somebody slips out and dies

because there is no one

to talk to.

bump, bump, bump.

It's not always easy to love and it takes courage to care. Strangely enough we are commanded to love. Jesus plainly said, "A new commandment I give unto you — that you love one another." Is love really commandable?

And we have a variety of ways of explaining what Jesus meant by "love one another." Even though He threw some additional light on the subject when He said everybody loves their loved ones — "I'm talking about loving your enemies also." Our stories go like this:

> I love you —
>> but I don't like you.
>> Or I love your soul —
>>> but your big old body and your personality
>>> just drive me up the wall.
> All the souls I ever saw were housed in bodies
> and amplified through personalities.

>> And somebody says, "I love you
>> 'in the Lord.'"
>> Like if you ever fall from grace
>> or fellowship then you're
>> the very first guy I mean to
>> drop from my list.
> And somebody says I love you —
>> enough to get to heaven —
> as if to say but as soon as we get there
> I'm gonna bust you in the mouth
>> or bend your halo
> or at least stomp on one of your wings.

But Jesus didn't seem to be talking about "get by" love or "get to heaven" love; He seemed to be speaking of love that was redemptive and changed people. Ann Kiemel is a young dean of women on a Christian college campus up in the Northeast and she is in demand all across the country as a speaker. Nearly every weekend she flys out somewhere to speak to groups of teens or young adults at retreats or conferences. She is certainly not an imposing speaker, preferring to sit quietly on a stool as she talks. The power is in what she says and believes. In her book, *I'm Out To Change My World,* she tells a story about a taxi driver down in Miami with whom she simply took a few moments to care:

It was in the summer
    and I got into a beat up old cab in Miami Beach
        and asked the old cab driver
    to take me to another hotel.
        It was hot
            and every window was rolled down
And I asked him,
    "What is the one word
        that describes your life?"
                "Can I give you two?"
                    he said.

He was old and gnarled,
    about as beat up as his cab.
"Yes," I said.
    "What are they?"
                "Bored
                    and unhappy."
"Sir,
    why are those the two words
that describe your life?"
                "I don't know.
                    I guess 'cause
                    I got nobody in the world."
"Nobody, Sir?
    No wife, no children, no family?

No one in the whole world for you?"
                "No."
"Tell me, Sir,
    how did you get to be an old man
and have nobody?"
                "'Cause I never got a
                good job and no woman
                wanted me."

"Sir,
can I sing you a song?"
"Sing?"
"I don't have a very good voice,
but I know you'd like my song."
"Just a minute, please."
He rolled up his window.
Then he nodded at me.

And I began to sing:

Something beautiful,
something good.
All my confusion,
He understood.
All I had to offer Him
was brokenness and strife.
But He's making something beautiful
out of my life.

"Sir,
do you know who I'm singing about?
Jesus Christ, He's the Lord of my life.
He laughs with me
and cries with me —"
"I'm a Jew."
"Sir, He'll walk with you,
He'll laugh with you.
He'll be your friend."
And just then we pulled under the portico of the next hotel
and I was fumbling in my purse for my money
when I saw this old hand reach out
and I let loose of the money in my purse.
I reached out and took his hand
almost afraid to look him in the eye
because I didn't know what he would say.
I lifted my eyes to his
and he was crying.
"Lady,
when I got in this old cab tonight

I was the loneliest person in the whole world.
I never heard anyone talk like you talked tonight
and I want your God.
He and I could ride together."

And I crawled out of that old cab
knowing that somewhere in Miami Beach
an old, gnarled, wrinkled man
drives a beat up old cab.
But he doesn't drive alone.
And I can hardly help but sing
when I know that the eternal God
is willing to invade an old cabbie's life
and love him.

Ralph Keyes, whose book I quoted earlier, told about something a friend of his had said in a poster design which has left a deep impression on me. I thought it was one of the best things in the book and he just stuck it in at the last as a footnote and you had to go way over in the back of the book to find it. I don't really like footnotes because I don't like to go chasing all over a book. I think if it's worth putting in — put it in. If it is not — don't, but don't make me roam from cover to cover to find a reference or a name or a statement especially if it is as good as this quote was. It reminds me of the old game kids used to play in hymnbooks. Turn to page 69 and when you got there, it said turn to page 248 and it chased you all through the book for some brilliant message on the last page you looked up.

But Keyes was so good that I went wherever he told me to in his book. He said:

"My friend, Howard Saunders, once designed
a calendar-poster entitled: The shortest distance
between two points is a straight line —
a straight line like, 'I need you,'
a straight line like, 'You really hurt me,'
a straight line like 'I haven't been honest with you,'
a straight line like, 'I love you.'

*Sometimes these words are so basic that we
take them for granted. But think about the
things that you wanted to say that were
left unsaid. To a parent who is gone. To
a lover who walked away. To a child who
ran away. Our hope for this new year
is to leave as little unsaid as we possibly can.
And maybe if we can influence the words
we write, then the printed word can begin
to shorten the distance between the
two points. The ending of my book is
obviously stolen from Howard. He's a good
person to steal an ending from."*

And I have been trying to care but more than that I have
been trying to express and to make that care known and
without exception the times that I have been able to break
out and do so have been the best moments of my day or week.

The other morning I had to have a blood test at the
doctor's office early in the morning. It was a UML20 or
something like that, that sounded pretty important anyway.
The only real problem, aside from the needle, is that you are
not allowed to eat or drink anything after midnight the night
before. So it really is kind of a surly crowd that gathers in
the office about 8:30 — some two hours before the doctor
who is making hospital calls — for these tests. Nobody's had
any breakfast or coffee or water, and there we sit —
stomachs growling, bad breath and the whole scene.

I had been there a few minutes when the nurse came to
the door and said, "Mrs. Smith and Mr. Benson." Now, I had
never had a blood test with a total stranger before, but we
started down the corridor — Mrs. Farmer, the nurse,
walking with Mrs. Smith and me trailing along behind.
Mrs. Farmer asked me how I was and I answered above my
growling stomach, "Fine," or "Gr-r-r-reat!" or "Fan-n-n-tastic!"
or something else inane and then she asked Mrs. Smith who
said, "I'm going mighty slow."

We were seated in the lab technician's office alone,
waiting on him to come, and being the whippy con-

versationalist that I am, I said to Mrs. Smith, "So you're going slow today." And her eyes welled up with tears and she replied, "Yes, I lost my mother over the weekend."

"Oh, I'm sorry — tell me a little about your Mom," and she told me how close they were and how although it had been expected someway, she just had not been prepared and she had had a very hard weekend.

About that time the technician came in and she was first and she told of having something I had never even heard of before, but she said it with such great pride I almost wished I had the same malady. "I have floating veins and it's really going to be hard to get blood from me." And sure enough, the technician poked and prodded and could not find a vein. Since her sleeves were short and tight he sent her up the hall to put on a hospital gown — one of the supreme indignities man heaps upon man, incidentally — and I was next and he got the blood.

And as I started up the hall, she was coming back down to the lab in the hospital gown, and I stopped and laid my hand on her arm for just a second. "I'm sorry about your Mom and I will be praying for you this week, especially, because I'm sure it will be a hard week for you." "Would you?" she said, through her tears. "Thank you so much."

I went on to the office and in the late afternoon flew to Kansas City to address a group of some two hundred choir directors. But as I laid my head on my pillow finally that night, it seemed to me the finest thing I had done all day — the thing that was the most Christlike — was to tell a lady I had never seen before, or for that matter, since — that I cared that she was brokenhearted.

I want to be involved in my world — with a prayer, with a smile, with whatever I have the Lord can use. Let me tell you something that really was fun for me that happened a few Sundays ago. I call it "Shoot-out On West Main."

> The two little boys in the back seat of a passing car
>   were firing away at me
>   with their new rifles.
> Their mom was undoubtedly hurrying home
>   to get the war out of the back seat

and into a larger theater of operations
      preferably out of ear shot
as I imagine by this time her ears were about shot.

But the redlight at Campus Drive caught her
and I pulled alongside them
    in front of the First Baptist Church.
I know it wasn't a very proper place for a shootout
but it was now or never.
   I calmly rolled down the window
   and took Patrick's cap pistol off the floor
where it had been left for just such emergencies

    (and because of Patrick's innate laziness)
  and began blazing away.
Amidst scattered return fire
    and squeals of delighted laughter
   they fell across the seats and into the floor
      in loud agonizing, prolonged deaths.

Just then the mother turned
  to see Grandfather Benson,
  forty-three years old,
  publisher, author, speaker,
  vice-president, manager
  and leader of men
firing away with an empty cap pistol
     at her two sons.
  She laughed
   and I did too, for
I was enormously pleased with myself.
  I had won a great battle
   right in front of my own wife and kids.
Except the dead were alive and well
    and firing away at the next three red lights
  (we have four in our town now)
I was pleased that just for a moment
   I had realized anew that
   I was a member of the family of man
  and had taken time out to play
    with a couple of my little brothers.

CHAPTER VII

CHAPTER VII

Do Something

I am believing more than ever that Jesus used love in His life and ministry for a couple of reasons. The first being that He is like the Father and the Father is love. He was love and could not fail to respond and react in that manner.

Secondly, I think this is true because it was and is the most powerful force there is in the world. Now I have been around the country and talked to enough people about this to know that this is not really a universally held and accepted idea. Most folk will admit that we ought to love but if the situation really calls for some positive, concrete action, then something more drastic than love will have to be done. It's like love is okay, but there are times when an effective step will have to be taken. More and more I am believing that there is nothing that is more effective or that is stronger than love.

I've talked with some district attorneys and some soldiers and some policemen and I know there have to be laws, and codes, and standards, and rules, and even radar, I guess, but even these work better in the context of courtesy and compassion. It is interesting how many things that take place in the headlines of the newspapers and we see on the six o'clock and ten o'clock news are about people who were doing things that were in essence acts that fairly screamed out, "Won't somebody please stop and look at me and listen to me and please, please, please, won't somebody care about what is happening to me!" Yes, I know that some things are cruel and sordid and are done by people who just seem hard and cold and beyond redemption, but I cannot be convinced that someone at the right time and place early in their lives could not have kept them from becoming hard and cold and cruel by loving and caring.

I have heard the idea expressed that love is a defense weapon or technique. No matter what it is that's going on about you, you can just fill your heart with love and sort of draw up within and keep sweet while the world surges about you in ruin. But love is more than a defensive, protective, "hide-behind" fortress into which we can retreat. It is also a positive, aggressive force that can be actively and energetically used to change circumstances and situations. I do not mean that it is a way to manipulate people or to get them to do what you want them to do but that it is the finest way to bring out the very best there is within a person.

This idea is exciting to me for a couple of reasons. The first is as I tried to point out in the last chapter, that it is the pivotal truth of the Bible and of the life of Christ.

The second reason is that I find this is a truth that is written more and more from a variety of viewpoints in many, many books. It is a good thing that the teachings of Jesus have passed into public domain and people cannot be sued for quoting Him and using His ideas without permission, because writers everywhere take the things He said and just write them down shamelessly as if they had thought of them all by themselves. I suspect that even part of this book is just a restatement of something He said long ago, at least I hope so.

Many of the books I read should really have Smith and Jones and Jesus on the cover and title page, because the ideas are mostly His. But most of the time His name is left off and it just says Smith and Jones.

Through my brains and intelligence and brilliance in choosing a father who was in the publishing business, I have by diligence and hard work achieved a management position in the company. Since I was not overly trained for this position except through experience, I have made a sincere effort to belong to enough management book clubs and to take enough magazines like *Fortune* and *Nation's Business* and *Business Week* to attempt to formulate some philosophy of management of my own. If nothing else, the books and magazines look very impressive lying around your office. But I have been trying to find out what it is that managers are supposed to do.

This often puzzles my children, also. The young ones ask, "What is it you do?" The truck drivers drive the truck, and the wrappers wrap the packages, and the key punch girls punch keys, and the typists type, and the artists design and illustrate — but what is it that you do? Patrick was supposed to go to work with me one day last fall and I was sick and he got himself a ride and went anyway. I was told later that he tried as best he could to do what he thought it was I did and he leaned back in my chair and put his feet on the desk and dialed the secretary to order cokes most of the day.

One of the things about management that I have found written in more and more books sounds strangely like something fresh out of the gospels. Roger D'Aprix in a book called *Struggle For Identity* was writing about the so-called "corporate tiger." This is the guy who will step on anybody and everybody in their headlong climb to the top. Mr. D'Aprix said, paraphrasing some words of Jesus,

> *"Perhaps the saddest thing about the corporate tiger is that his sole cause in life is usually his own career, his own personal ambitions. Once he learns through experience and training to detach himself from such single-mindedness and to define himself as a minister to the people about him, then and only then will he truly be of value to himself and his organization."*

Another has said that you are "a feeling human being first and a manager second." Part of what I am supposed to do each day is to walk through the building and know as many of our people as I possibly can by their names and to be able to ask them about their wives and families and dreams as well as why they are not doing their jobs better.

And I am believing that openness and compassion and love are the best ways to run a business. And because we have a team of younger guys who feel this way, also, I think that our company is a redemptive place to work. We have an old building and there are times when everybody wants the one old elevator and it is a growing company and there are times when everybody wants their job out of the art department next. And there are times when tempers flare and people exchange words they should not have said. They even accuse me from time to time of getting the "tight-whites" which means that when I start through the building with my lips tight and drawn, it is time to get in your own area and get on with your job. I'm not saying that it is a perfect place to work but I am saying that the heartening sign is that when these things happen you will almost invariably find whoever had the "tight-whites" retracing his steps in a half-hour or so to apologize for what he said, and the way he said it.

> So I want to say firmly —
> that's whispering for me — remember,
> love is the way to run a business.
> What about the bottom line,
> what about the ratio of the earnings
> to investment,
> what are sales compared to last year,
> what is the age of the receivables,
> how often does the inventory turn —
> I know these are questions that must be answered
> but they are just effects
> not causes —
> a business is people
> people who create product with other people

product to be ordered, and inventoried
to be wrapped, shipped, delivered
by people
to people who sell to other people —
a business is people
and people respond best always
to love.

If you really want to lose some money on a given day, go
chew somebody out in bookkeeping or shipping or
somewhere in your building. Do it in front of everybody
else and then see how much work you get for your money
the rest of the day from that person or the rest of the
people who were so embarrassed for him and mad at you
that the whole afternoon is spent in mumbling and
grumbling about what a sorry place this is to work anyway.

I read about a man who said he never fussed at an
employee in the afternoon because he liked dogs. He went
on to explain that usually what happened was the man went
home frustrated and fuming and the first thing he did was to
give his wife a few short answers and this made her mad
also. About that time the oldest son innocently strolls
through the kitchen and mom gives him a verbal blast.
He then seeks out his sister and passes it on. In a little while
the baby brother comes wandering in and the sister tells him
in no uncertain terms to let her things alone and stay out of
the room. And the poor little brother, being the low man on
the totem pole, starts out into the yard and the dog is asleep
on the back step so he just kicks the dog. So the employer
didn't bawl people out in the afternoon because he liked dogs.

And if it is true that anger and frustration can be and is
readily passed along, then how much more true it is that love
and kindness can run through a whole company and family.

But how do you start? I've had people who said if I went
and told my foreman that I loved him, he would think I was
crazy or, in the case of a man telling a man, he might just
get slugged in the mouth. I don't know exactly where or
how you can start, but somehow, in some way, whether you
are the boss, or the accounting department manager or a

worker on the dock, you must begin — by word, by a hand on a shoulder, by interest, by bearing burdens, by smiling, by bringing an extra piece of cake — you must let the people around you at work know that you care. And you can begin to transform a department or an area by love, whether you are the supervisor or the newest person there.

Yes, people have to be motivated, and some people will give you 110 percent and some will give you about 63 and occasionally someone will have to be let go, but compassion and concern will go further in these situations and any other than all of the other strategies like fussing, and ranting, and staying on somebody's back all the time that we often use instead for:

"love is the way to run a business"

Lean way over close to me now, because I am fixing to say something that means even more to me than what I have just been trying to express:

"love is the way to raise a family."

and the family is just about the place where I want to succeed the most. In fact, I feel that if I fail here, my life will have been a failure in spite of anything else I may accomplish, and if I can succeed here, it will somehow atone for all the other failures of my whole life. My most often and fervent prayer is that I will be a successful father. I love to sing the song "I Have Decided To Follow Jesus":

> *I have decided to follow Jesus,*
> *I have decided to follow Jesus,*
> *I have decided to follow Jesus,*
> *No turning back —*
> *No turning back.*

And I like the verse:

> *Take this world but give me Jesus,*
> *Take this world but give me Jesus,*
> *Take this world*
> *but give me Jesus*
> *No turning back —*
> *No turning back.*

But when they come to the last verse I have to drop out because I cannot sing:

> *If none go with me, still I will follow,*
> *If none go with me, still I will follow.*
> *If none go with me, still I will follow,*
> *No turning back —*
> *No turning back.*

I can't sing it — if I live in such a way that I must go by myself — with absolutely no criticism of anyone else and the way they have raised their family…, then I think I feel like Moses must have felt when he told the Lord, "If the children don't get to go to Canaan, then blot my name out of the book, too."

I was reading somewhere of a retreat for career men and at the end of the weekend the last thing each man was to do was to write a headline that he would most like to see in the paper about himself and one man wrote: Henry Smith Was Elected Father Of The Year Today — His Wife And Family Were The Judges.

> In the midst of constant provision
> for clothes, discipline, braces, and hamburgers,
> a parent's real priority must always be
> to instill dreams, ideals, thoughts, beliefs
> of dignity, beauty, self-control, service
> and most important of all, to impart faith.

> One does the best one can by precept and pattern
> but all too quickly the time speeds by;
> where do they go, the days and the decades,
> days so filled with goodness —
> we lived them like they'd always be —
> days that brought such tiredness and hurt
> we thought they would not pass
> and days when we scarcely knew
> whether to laugh or cry because they marked
> both beginnings and endings.

> Yesterday they were solely dependent on us —
> now they have a sturdy resilience of their own.
> Not long ago he wanted a trike,

and now he has his drivers license.
Yesterday she was a baby—
today she is a Brownie,
tomorrow a college freshman,
and the next day a bride.
Where do they go, the days and the decades?

How could he have a son of his own
when we just brought him home from the hospital,
and why do we insist on calling the littlest one
the baby when he is in the third grade?
And how could I be forty-three when I
am just barely thirty?
Where do they go, the days and the decades?

They speed by and you stand aside to see
if their deeds and accomplishments
reflect the things in which you most believed.
Will they do the right, will they choose the best
no longer because of punishment or reprisal
but because deep within their own hearts
they have made those things their own.

Stumbling along the path of parenthood
one at times tries to stuff these things
down unwilling and resisting throats
when they should have been gently
loved into another's being.

I am a believer that the only way to even begin to try to be
a parent is with the use of the power of love. We have tried
a variety of ways of disciplining our children. When they were
small enough, we could give them a quick swat on the rear
end. And there were times when I felt that all the nerve
endings that had to do with hearing, quietness, muscle con-
trol and other vital signs were centered in that general area
of the body where they sat down. And I must admit
there were times when I felt it worked. We used to have a
Volkswagen and when things weren't going right in the back
seat, you could backhand everybody including Peggy with
one stroke of your arm. I was the biggest and they couldn't

hit me back or if they did it was only on the kneecap and didn't hurt too much.

But then they get bigger. I used to wrestle Bobby and Mike and then Mike and I used to wrestle Bob. I try not to wrestle with any of them now. If I wanted to discipline Mike today by paddling him, I would have to say, "Mike — Sir — how would you like to bend over so I can bring you into line?" Because when he is standing up straight he is taller than I am.

When the older boys hit the teens we tried grounding them once or twice, you know. "You can't leave the yard all weekend except to go to church." I don't know who gets the worse end of that deal — the "groundee" or the "groundor." I just know it doesn't make for much of a weekend with an unhappy boy or two sitting around. And anyway it really won't work because if they are old enough and mad enough they will just leave home.

Well, you can cut off their allowance, but who needs $2.00 a week anyway. So what do you do — ignore them, just keep your head in the newspaper until they get their hair cut — what do you do? I believe the most powerful step you can take is to turn the fervor of your love up another ten degrees.

The rumors were that Mike was in some trouble —
first they came from school
and then of course they grew more rampant
in the fertile soil of the church.

And so we called a family council — Peg and I
"What are you going to do about it?" she said,

"Well, what are *you* going to do about it?" was my reply.
Will we confront him,
will we ask him,
will we assume he didn't
and treat him like he did
will we accuse him,
will we subtly tighten the reins of his freedom
until he "cracks" and it
becomes evident as to the truth of the rumors?

Now Peg is more of the
"let's get this all out in the open now" type
and I through my natural wisdom, intelligence
and cowardice am generally willing to
avoid, postpone, and run from all the confrontations,
crises and summit meetings
that I possibly can.
Unfortunately this time she chose to defer to me
as the leader of the home
and turned the matter over to me.

"What are you going to do if it is not true?"
I am going to continue to go into his room
at night and kneel by his bed—
(he sleeps on his stomach)
and I am going to rub his back for a moment
and say, "Mike, I love you
and I'm proud to be your Dad
I hope you sleep well
I'll see you in the morning
goodnight."

"And what are you going to do if it *is* true?"
I am going to continue to go into his room
at night and kneel by his bed—
(he sleeps on his stomach)
and I am going to rub his back for a moment
and say, "Mike, I love you
and I'm proud to be your Dad
I hope you sleep well
I'll see you in the morning
goodnight."

It was a couple of months later
he came first to his mom
and then a week or so later to me and said,
"I was in some trouble at school
but I got it worked out
I'm sorry as I can be
and it won't happen again—"

I believe that love —
steady, patient, unceasing,
deep, expressed, oozed —
is the only reliable option open to parents —
It's better than advice, grounding, cutting the allowance,
paddlings, punishments, threats,
or any other of the dozens of dodges and ruses we work —
on our unsuspecting and waiting children.
Just care, just love, just show it.
DO SOMETHING.

So we were doubly proud the other day
when he wrote from school
"Send me my Bible
I'm running for freshman class chaplain."
We did and he is.

Love is the way to run a home. I don't mean the "go in
your room and keep sweet because your heart is filled with
love" love — I mean "the force which binds you so loosely
together that everyone can be themselves and so tightly that
no one can get away" love. Love that just loves, the Jesus
kind of love, the love that is so strongly implied in the
"sharing of the very being of God."

Kids are smart, you know, and they know what's going on.
A couple of years ago we were riding along on a trip and our
kids began to compile a glossary of oft-used parental
expressions. It was one of those kind of times when you were
laughing to keep from crying. Some of it went like this:

"we'll see" — a term which means the same as "I'll
think about it"

"I'll think about it" — a term which means "maybe"

"maybe" — a term which means no further action on
the matter will be taken.

"convention" — a term which means Mom and Dad are
in Florida and we are with a
babysitter

"tomorrow" — a term used to express increments
of time from a minimum of

thirty days until never

"ask your daddy" — a term which means *no* but it's
his turn to tell you.

"ask your mother" — another term which means *no* but
it's her turn to tell you.

You're not fooling them a bit. They know you're bewildered
and confused and don't know all the answers and they know
that the louder you say something, the less sure you are that
it is right. They know that sometimes when you are shouting
at them, it is because you are mad at someone else and it
has nothing to do with them except they are in the unhappy
position of not being able to answer back, but they will forgive you, if over the days and months you have made it
unmistakably clear that you love them very, very much. They
will accept your errors as errors of your head and of your
judgment if they can only be sure that there was nothing
anywhere in your heart except boundless, limitless love
for them.

We have a warm, open, outgoing affection at our house.
I really have to give Peggy most of the credit for this. I came
from a reserved family. We Bensons were "cool." We loved
each other and we knew it, so we didn't have to go around
drumming it into each other's ears all the time. Peg's family
was a little different in that they celebrated everybody's
birthday and Mother's Day and Father's Day and nearly any
other day that seemed like it was half reasonable for cele-
brating. And Peg brought this warmth to our place. You can't
even mention something one of the kids did or said without
this warm look with the glistening eyes covering her face.

And to me our house is the finest place in the world to
be because there is love and warmth and fellowship. Not
always harmony, but always love and fellowship. We don't
go to bed at night until we have all hugged and kissed and
said I love you two or three times to each other. And .
nobody goes away in the morning without getting several
"have a good day's" and "I love you's." There are a lot of
Bensons and it takes awhile to get all that in, I know, but I
think it is the most effective way there is for parents to raise

children and incidentally it is also a very, very effective way
for kids to raise parents.

We live out a ways from town — 25 miles or so from where
I work and it is not inconceivable on a busy week for me to
leave home in the morning before the kids are up and get
home after they are asleep. I have lived in my house for four
or five days and never had a meal with my kids or even
seen them awake.

However, I so strongly believe in the power of love that
I don't care what time I come in at night or how long they
have been asleep — I don't go to bed myself until I have made
my rounds. First I go up into Tom and Patrick's room. Tom
sleeps on the top bunk and I catch his chin and turn his face
toward me and look at those blond curls and his fair skin.
He's a heavy sleeper and you couldn't wake him if you tried,
and he doesn't even know I'm there but I say, "Tom Benson,
you rascal, I love you. I thought of you a lot today and
everytime I did, I smiled."

And then I kneel down by the bottom bunk where Patrick
is asleep. He is eight and the baby of the family and enjoys
every minute of it. I don't know when he's going to grow up
but the way they grow up so fast anyway, I'm not pushing
him. I don't care if he takes his teddy bear to college. And
he sleeps with any assortment of stuffed animals. If I can
reach in and finally find the one that is Patrick, I remind
him that I am so very proud to be his father and that I love
him very much.

And I cross the hall to Leigh's room and she isn't quite
so sound a sleeper. She always returns my hug and my
expression of love. "You are so fine, Leigh, and I love you"
and groggily the pronouns are reversed and it comes right
back, "You are fine, too, Daddy, and I love you, too."

Then I nearly always stop in a room downstairs where I
used to have a study. It's a sad room to me because when
you're the oldest and the biggest and you aren't afraid of the
dark anymore you move down there. It is almost a sort of a
launching pad because when they move down there you
know the next move is out — to college or to their own
apartment or house. But I go down there and "love" across

the city to 160 Woodmont Boulevard where Bob and Debbie and Robert the III live and then across 700 miles into Oklahoma where Mike is in a crazily jumbled up dormitory room. I say, "Mike, I love you and am praying for good days for you."

Why do you do that when they are asleep or far away, you ask? Because of two things: I want to "share in the very being of God" and because I think it is the noblest and wisest thing I can do as a parent. And it is doubly effective at our house because Peg has already made the rounds before me.

Between us we want to stuff into the "awares" and the "unawares" of the lives of our children as many smiles, songs, kisses, "I love you's" and deeds of love as we possibly can.

One night I bent over and kissed Patrick on the cheek and quickly stood up and started out of the room. I was so tired it was about the last "get up" I had left for the whole day, I thought, when he stopped me cold and brought me back to his bedside:

"Why do you kiss me so fast?"

And why do we let the finest, most precious moments of our lives go by without a word thinking tomorrow or on our vacation there'll be time to hike and swim and love our children. Why do we withhold from them the very thing they need the most—ourselves and our love.

The time to love is now. The time to begin is right now. I have actually talked to parents who say it never occurred to them to tell their children they love them and I think some of the most effective things I have ever done in retreats and conventions is to send people back home to express their love to their kids.

It was a bright sunshiny morning—
the first day of ten days off for me—
and I was out in the yard early—
working on a wall down at the lake.
Knee deep in the pleasant, warm water
I could hardly have been happier or more at peace.

Patrick came down and began to throw rocks in the water.
You don't have to teach little boys to throw rocks
they just seem to be born both with the
skill and the desire.

He wanted me to stop and play with him.
"Teach me how to make them skip."
"In a little while," I said,
"let me get a little more of this wall built."
After awhile he got tired of waiting
and started up the hill to the house.

I figured he'd be back in a few minutes,
but later in the morning when I went up for a drink
he was in the bed with a high fever.
It turned out to be a very serious illness
that was to spread through the whole family—
not to mention my vacation.
It took some of us to the hospital
and all of us to bed.
Fortunately for us it was all over
in a month or so,
having run its course with no lingering effects;
and there have been other days
and other chances to skip rocks with "Pack"—

But I can still see him trudging
up that hill—a long pull for his short legs
and I'm reminded that you never know
they're coming back—
there aren't any guarantees
and the only time you really know
you can skip rocks
is when you're saying "in a little while."

CHAPTER VIII

CHAPTER VIII

Come Share The Being

We have been thinking about some deep truths. To me they are challenging and I would like to hope that I am in the process of discovering and appropriating them for my very own.

But very frankly, just between you and me, although I believe that God is life and that all the world exists and is sustained by his life there are times, too many times, when I feel lifeless and dull and drab. And I know that I am not reflecting "the life of God" very well to those about me. I don't feel very much like a breath of fresh air or a ray of sunlight. Sometimes by the end of the day I feel like being carried from the car to the house so that I can take a nap in front of the TV to rest up for the long trip to our bedroom on the second floor. And yet I cannot feel that this is the way I am supposed to be and that I am "sharing in the very being of God."

And to be just as frank, it is not always easy to love. I still am affected periodically by the "tight-whites" and on more occasions than I would like to admit, I find myself letting someone have it. Verbally, of course, not physically. I never

ever get mad enough to swap rights with anyone. Even when I am not a lover, I never have any desire to be a fighter.

Now, I wouldn't necessarily be admitting these things if it were not for the fact that it probably is a language that even you may understand.

I have been quoting a word in the phrase that I have been using, but up to now, I haven't said anything about it. But I am beginning to see its relation to the whole and want to write a little bit about it now. You remember the phrase is "to share in the very being of God" and we have been thinking together about the "being" part. And that is really an exciting, challenging prospect. Then one afternoon I saw a word up at the front of the phrase that put "life and love" and "His being" within my reach. I don't know how I overlooked it for so long—probably you've already seen it and its significance.

The word is "share."

The word itself is used a lot these days. People who come to speak to other groups of people say they have come to share. It usually means I have come to tell you what I know, but if you want to talk back to me or "share" with me what you know, I'm sorry but I have a plane to catch. To share has come to mean to transmit information. It really has several deeper meanings. One is that there is no real communication or sharing unless there is trust and empathy. Probably if a manager of a company has to exhort his people to communicate better with each other, the problem is deeper than a failure to move information back and forth. It is more likely that the group has lost the all important feeling that they are all in this thing together. The American Heritage Dictionary of the English Language defines part of the meaning of "share" as follows:

> to share: to participate in, to use, or
> experience in common; to have or
> take a part.

All of a sudden it dawned on me that God was saying to me, "Why don't you take what you have and what you are—

your being — and I will take what I have and what I am — my
being — and we will share, we will participate in, we will use,
we will experience together in common."

And I began to see that as fantastic as I am, witty, knowl-
edgeable, leader of men, talented — as great as I am — when I
put what I had and was and am and hope to be with what
He is, that all of a sudden, I had stumbled on to the bargain
of a lifetime. I was getting the long end of the stick.

Do you remember when they had
old fashioned Sunday school picnics?
It was before air-conditioning.
They said, "We'll meet at Sycamore Lodge
in Shelby Park at 4:30 Saturday.

You bring your supper and we'll furnish the tea."
But you came home at the last minute
and when you got ready
to pack your lunch,
all you could find in the refrigerator
was one dried up piece of baloney
and just enough mustard in the bottom of the jar
so that you got it all over your knuckles
trying to get to it.
And there were just two stale pieces of bread.
So you made your baloney sandwich
and wrapped it in some brown bag
and went to the picnic.

And when it came time to eat
you sat at the end of a table and spread
out your sandwich.
But the folks next to you — the lady was a good cook
and she had worked all day
and she had fried chicken, and baked beans,
and potato salad, and homemade rolls,
and sliced tomatoes,
and pickles, and olives, and celery,
and topped it off with
two big homemade chocolate pies.

And they spread it all out beside you
and there you were with your baloney sandwich.
But they said to you,
"Why don't we put it all together?"
"No, I couldn't do that, I just couldn't even think of it,"
you murmured embarrassedly.
"Oh, come on, there's plenty of chicken
and plenty of pie, and plenty of everything—
and we just love baloney sandwiches.
Let's just put it all together."
And so you did and there you sat—
eating like a king
when you came like a pauper.

And I get to thinking—I think of me "sharing" with God. When I think of how little I bring, and how much He brings and that He invites me to "share," I know I should be shouting to the housetops, but I am so filled with awe and wonder that I can hardly be heard.

I know you don't have enough love or faith, or grace, or mercy or wisdom—there's just not enough to you. But He has—He has all those things in abundance and says, "Let's just put it all together."

Consecration, denial, sacrifice, commitment, crosses these were kind of hard, flinty words to me, until I saw it in the light of "sharing." Not just me kicking in what I have because God is the biggest kid in the neighborhood and wants it all for Himself. But He is speaking to me and saying, "Everything that I possess is available to you. Everything that I am and can be to a person, I will be to you."

When I think about it like that, it really amuses me to see somebody running along through life hanging on to their dumb bag with that stale baloney sandwich in it, saying, "God's not to get my sandwich! No sirree, this is mine!" Did you ever see anybody like that —so needy—just about half-starved to death, hanging on for dear life. It's not that He needs your sandwich—the fact is, you need His chicken.

And this matter of "sharing," of releasing what you have is simply a recognition of the most basic fact of life. There is no

way to hold on. Life, friends, loved ones must be held with
an "open hand." All attempts to clutch, grasp, hold tightly
are just fruitless, empty gestures. Life gives with a generous
hand, but it also takes away.

He was once a tall man
he was energetic, active —
he loved people, places, life itself.
He teased, smiled, laughed with folk.
He was a self-made man —
had his own business and ran it well.
He had sold it to provide a retirement income
and often told his wife,
"We'll have enough to keep us
if we're careful."

But he was old now and lay a-dying,
a pitiful, bundle of skin and bones.
It seemed almost a sacrilege to be there
as he made the last short journey of his life.
He would have been so embarrassed
for he was always so courtly,
well-dressed, clean-shaven, princely —
but there he lay — no longer feeling,
seeing, hearing, or caring —
his total energies and efforts
given over to gasping for breath,
a habit deeply engrained, having
begun nearly eighty years before,
when with a pat on the bottom
and a wail he had first
gulped air into his lungs.

It is rather remarkable how much alike
our comings and our goings are —
if disease, accident, or so-called "untimely death"
don't keep us from our appointments
with old age, infirmity, and helplessness.
He was as helpless now as he had
been those first moments of his life.

There is a sense in which it seems unfair —
　　just as we begin to find
　　self-reliance, independence, autonomy,
　　it slowly begins to ebb away.
Just about the time the kids are on their own
and the thirty-year mortgage
　　　　　has only four months longer to run,
　　　　　　they give you the dinner and watch
and tell you they'll never forget you
and some twenty-two-year-old
　　　　　is at your desk the next morning
　　　　　doing your job — sometimes better —
and breath comes shorter,
　　　　　　　　and pain comes éasier,
　　　　and steps get steeper,
　　　　and print gets smaller.

In a way it's a kind of mockery
　　　　　　unless deep down inside you
　　　　　you begin to realize that the
　　　　　hands that put you here
　　　　have not abandoned you to the capriciousness
　　　　　　of nature or the folly of others
　　　　　but that all the time they are guiding
　　　you along paths of order and design.
Maybe we enter life the way we do
　　　　　so that no man can ever say
　　　　　　　　"I got here by myself"
　　　and just maybe we depart
　　　　　in the same manner, so one will always
　　　faintly sense that he alone
　　　　is not adequate within himself.

Jesus knew this secret of "openhanded" living. I know He
didn't own a car or a house or a color TV, so He wasn't
worried about much of the "clutter" that we are. But He had
friends and a family, and He loved life. Sometimes people say
they can't follow Christ because they love life too much. As
if to say He didn't. But He seemed to have loved it more

than we do — He noticed breezes, and mustard seeds, and fields white unto harvest and sowers going out to sow, and shepherds climbing out on cliffs to rescue lambs. He noticed lonely fathers whose young sons had left home and He noticed young sons who were homesick and proud and miserable. He loved life, but He held it with an open hand.

And He talked of paradoxes — paradoxes that can only be explained when you superimpose commitment and consecration against "sharing in the very being of God." There's just no other way to explain "the first shall be last and the last shall be first" and "he that would be the leader, let him be the servant." For it is only in love — "sharing" love that two beings become one and yet remain two; it is only in dying that we live; it is only in letting go that we really hold.

I guess one of my favorite scenes in the whole Bible is in the last chapter of John's gospel. The disciples had fished all night and Jesus stood on the shore and had a fire ready to cook their breakfast. And after they ate, Jesus began to talk to Peter about his love. It was an extra poignant moment because it was one of these last moments — when there wasn't time to just chat or visit. You remember the story and how finally the third time for emphasis, Jesus had asked him, "Do you love me more than these?"

> Peter was sitting on the shoreline of his life —
> there was the sea,
> there was the boat and the nets —
> the fish were there,
> the smell of the sea air
> the gulls overhead.
> And down the beach a ways
> was the village where he had been raised.
> His family was there — his friends.
> All of his world —
> everything he had known and loved
> was within the sight and sound
> of his ears and eyes that morning
> and the question was squarely put —
> more than these?

I like his answer — "Lord, you know everything —
everything I think,
every corner of my heart —
I have no secrets from you —
and Lord, you know
I love you."

It seems to be universal among believers, although we do
not always all describe it or give it the same terminology, to
tell of the time when Jesus stands on the shoreline of your
life and the question is:

"Do you love me more than these?"

I was in the hospital some time ago on a rather routine
matter, when the doctors came and said, "This no longer is
routine — it's serious and it doesn't look good at all. You can
go home a couple of weeks for Christmas but you'll need to
check back in on the 28th for surgery and after that we can
give you some better idea of the problem you are facing."

And so I went home for Christmas. I was with *my* wife, and
my children in *my* house, but during that time I realized that
I might have to make good on something I had been giving
lip service to for a long time. Long ago I had placed them in
God's hands but I was holding on pretty tight. And as I began
to release my grip on them and place them in His care I
began to own them in a way that I never had known before
and their smiles, their words, their presence had new and
richer meaning to me than ever before. And these days since
that opening of my hand have been the richest and finest of
my life — mostly I think because I began to get into perspec-
tive the stewardship-ownership truth that underlies life.

Go ahead — eat your baloney sandwich, as long as you can.
But when you can't stand its tastelessness or drabness any
longer, when you get so tired of running your own life by
yourself and doing it your way and figuring out all the answers
with no one else to help when trying to accumulate,
hold, grasp, and keep everything together in your own strength
gets to be too big a load, when you begin to realize
that by yourself you're never going to be able to fulfill your
dreams, I hope you'll remember that it doesn't have to be

that way at all — you have been invited to "share in the very
being of God." Not commanded to give up and die or to be
beaten to your knees but to "share in His life and love
and grace."

It is a relationship that does not grow out of fear; it comes
about as we sense our need and his infinite resources; it
happens as we are moved by gratitude and love.

I never really sat down and said,
I'm going to work so hard and long
that I won't have any time for my
family at home.
But sometimes that's the way it happens
until you skip across the line
that subtly divides your owning a business
and a business owning you.
It seemed I had been gone so much —
so many nights and weekends
that I didn't feel like I deserved
the title "Dad" or much less
the love and happiness with which it was bestowed.

So I got up early one Saturday morning
determined to earn the price of admission
back into my family again.
Tom had been building a tree house.
He explained to his mother it was the kind
you sat under instead of in.
It was some old boards leaning against the tree.
This morning I went to work,
and by the time Tom came out
into the morning sunlight
I had the floor in for a genuine
up-the-tree, enter by ladder only,
sit-up-in kind of tree house.
Tom looked up into these trees
at that tree house —
only about six feet up because
I'm afraid of heights and
anyway, it makes my nose bleed —

and he looked at his "lean to"
and then he looked at me
and took me by the hand
and just blurted out, "Gee, Dad,
I wouldn't care if me and you
was the only two people in the world."

And I suspect that when you or when I really learn what it means to live with an open hand, we will have said something like Tom said, or something like Peter said. And I believe we also will have discovered that when we share with Him —

We are always more —
never less
Always better —
never worse
He doesn't come to
divide or subtract —
He always adds and multiplies
so that whatever it was that we were going to be —
with Him it will exceed our fondest dreams
"to come to share in the very being of God."